Editor
Eric Migliaccio

Illustrator
Mark Mason

Cover Artist
Brenda DiAntonis

Editor in Chief
Ina Massler Levin, M.A.

Creative Director
Karen J. Goldfluss, M.S. Ed.

Art Production Manager
Kevin Barnes

Art Coordinator
Renée Christine Yates

Imaging
Rosa C. See

Publisher
Mary D. Smith, M.S. Ed.

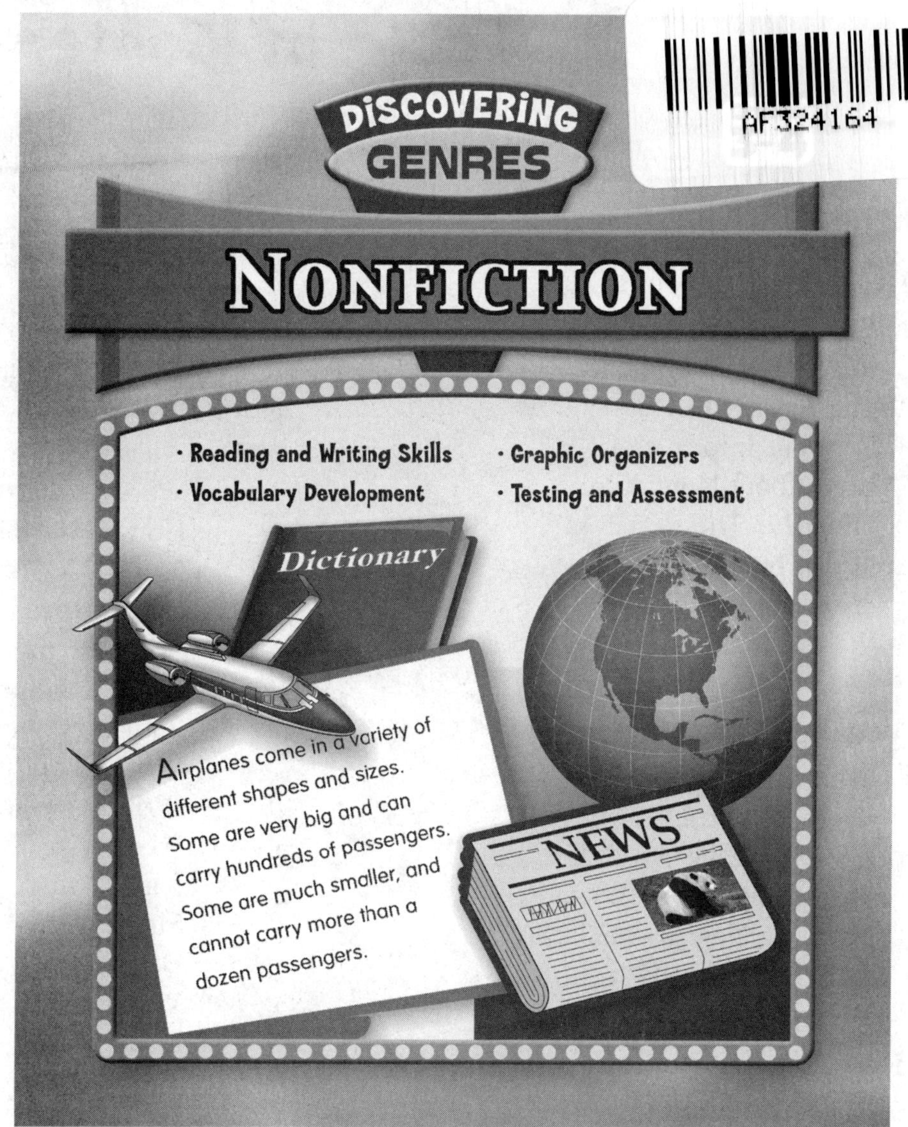

Author

Susan Mackey Collins, M. Ed.

Teacher Created Resources, Inc.
6421 Industry Way
Westminster, CA 92683
www.teachercreated.com
ISBN: 978-1-4206-9050-7

© 2008 Teacher Created Resources, Inc.
Made in U.S.A.

Table of Contents

Table of Contents *(cont.)*

Introduction

Literature is such a wonderful part of language arts. When students are tired of learning about commas and capitalization or spelling and synonyms, there is always a special story sitting somewhere on a shelf, just waiting to grab the imagination and take each one of us on a wonderful adventure. This book, *Discovering Genres: Nonfiction,* is the perfect companion piece to that adventure.

There are so many different genres available to anyone who wants to read. Sometimes understanding these different story types can take a bit of extra effort. Many people find a certain type or genre can be more enjoyable if the reader has some background knowledge about the type of book he or she is reading.

This series of books is designed to help anyone interested in reading better and understanding better the variety of genres of literature.

This book was also written with the wide range of ability levels of third- and fourth-grade students in mind. Both teachers and parents can benefit from the variety of activities provided in this book. A parent can use the book to work with his or her child at home and to help provide a better understanding of a particular genre. Similarly, a teacher can select pages that provide additional explanation for the class about nonfiction. Both parents and teachers will find the book has been divided into several helpful sections:

- Define and Recognize
- Vocabulary Development
- Reading Strategies
- Writing Skills
- Grammar Connections
- Test Practice and Assessment
- Culminating Projects
- Graphic Organizers

The practice of reading should be an enjoyable experience for all children. By practicing vital reading skills and being exposed to a variety of genres, students will have a positive experience as they prepare for a lifetime of reading.

Meeting Standards *(cont.)*

Each lesson in *Discovering Genres: Nonfiction, Grades 3–4* meets one or more of the
following standards, which are used with permission from McREL. (Copyright 2000
McREL, Mid-continent Research for Education and Learning. Telephone: 303-337-0990.
Website: *www.mcrel.org.*)

Language Arts Standards	Page Numbers
• Using reading skills and strategies to understand a variety of literary passages and texts	5–23, 37–38, 44–48, 64, 77–79, 107, 111, 115–119, 121, 125, 129
• Understands similarities and differences within and among literary works from various genres and cultures (e.g., settings, character types, events, point of view, role of natural phenomena)	24–26, 31–36, 39–43, 49–50, 69, 103–104, 108–110, 112–113
• Uses the general skills and strategies of the writing process	51–57, 61–63, 65–68, 70–76 100–102, 105–06, 114, 120, 122–124, 127, 130–139, 141–144
• Uses prewriting strategies to plan written work (e.g., uses graphic organizers, story maps, and webs; groups related ideas; takes notes; brainstorms ideas; organizes information according to type and purpose of writing)	27, 29–30, 58–60,126, 128, 140, 145–165
• Uses grammatical and mechanical conventions in written compositions	28, 80–99

What It Is

Nonfiction writing is writing that has real people, places, and settings. Some nonfiction writing reads almost like a novel, but the characters, setting, and plot in a nonfiction book are all real.

Nonfiction writing is filled with information. Textbooks, reference books, letters, diaries, and news stories are all examples of nonfiction writing.

Many students enjoy reading nonfiction. It is fun to find out more information about something you really like. You may love to skateboard. If so, there are nonfiction books that teach you more about skateboarding. Maybe you like to cook. There are plenty of nonfiction books to teach you about this, too. Whatever your interests, there is probably a nonfiction book just waiting to be read by you!

Directions: Write the correct answer on the lines provided.

1. What is nonfiction? ____

____

2. Nonfiction writing is filled with ___________________________________

3. Give three examples of nonfiction writing: ___________________________

____

____

4. What is something you enjoy doing? ________________________________

Do you think there might be a nonfiction book written about this topic? _________

Something Extra: With your teacher's or librarian's help, see if you can find a nonfiction book on the topic you wrote about in question #4. In the box below, write the title of the book you found.

Recognizing Nonfiction

Nonfiction writing is so much fun to read. Nonfiction writing gives you information about real people, places, and things. You can learn so much when you read writing that is about real things.

What if you always wanted to know more about turtles? A nonfiction book on turtles can teach you all kinds of interesting facts. You might learn where turtles live, what they eat, or even how long they live.

There are many nonfiction books available to anyone who wants to read them. Next time you go to the library, be sure to check out a nonfiction book—you just might learn something exciting and new!

Directions: Below are some nonfiction and fiction statements about turtles. Remember, *nonfiction* means the statement is true. *Fiction* means the statement is not true.

If the statement is nonfiction, write the word **True** on the line. If the statement is fiction, write **False** on the line.

Helpful Hint: You may have to do some research to be sure your answer is correct.

_____________ **1.** Turtles pull their heads into their shells to protect themselves.

_____________ **2.** One type of turtle is a sea turtle.

_____________ **3.** Turtles live in or near water.

_____________ **4.** All turtles like to play on swings and slides.

_____________ **5.** Many turtles wear sunglasses to protect their eyes from the sun.

_____________ **6.** Turtles are reptiles.

_____________ **7.** Turtles only eat insects if they are covered in chocolate.

_____________ **8.** Some types of turtles can be found in the Atlantic Ocean.

The Library Helper

Go to the library to help you learn more about nonfiction books.

Directions: Have your teacher or librarian show you where the nonfiction books are located. Then answer the questions that follow.

1. Are the nonfiction books organized alphabetically? ______________________

2. Nonfiction books in the library are divided with a number system. Certain types of books fall under certain numbers. This system is known as the Dewey Decimal System. Go to the 300 section and list the titles of two books in this section.

   A. ____

   B. ____

3. Go to the Reference section of the library. These are also nonfiction books. What type of books do you find in the Reference section? ______________________

   ____

4. In which section of the library would you find books about sports?

   ____

5. In which section of the library would you find books about different countries?

   ____

For Your Information

One type of nonfiction writing is *informational* or *reference* nonfiction. To help you understand this term, you need to understand what information is.

> *Information = facts provided or learned about something or someone*

What if you had never heard of the word *chimney*? If you want to find out what a chimney is, you would need information. You might ask these questions:

- *Is it a person, place, or thing?*
- *Have you ever seen one?*
- *What does it do?*
- *Does anyone you know have one?*

You would need to gather information to find out what a chimney is. You might use a dictionary to look up the word. You might talk to other people and ask if they know what a chimney is. Or, you might use some other sources to help you find out what the word means.

When an author writes informational or reference nonfiction, this means he is writing something that will give information; and the information should be true. The word *nonfiction* means the information is not made up or false; it is real. Reference books such as dictionaries and encyclopedias are great sources of informational nonfiction. Some resources on the computer also give great informational nonfiction.

Directions: Use an encyclopedia, dictionary, or the Internet (with an adult's permission) to help you find the information below.

1. Which two countries touch or border the United States of America?

   ___________________________________   ___________________________________

2. What is a *chimney*? ____

   ____

3. Where do polar bears live? ____

4. What is the definition of *octagon*? _____________________________________

Nuts About Nonfiction

Student Directions

Nonfiction writing is writing that has real people, places, and settings. Most nonfiction writing gives the reader lots of information. Textbooks, reference books, directions, warning labels, and brochures are all examples of nonfiction.

To put it in a nutshell: nonfiction is writing that gives information about real people, places, or things.

Materials:

- glue
- scissors
- crayons
- the "Acorns" worksheet (page 11)
- the "Squirrels" worksheet (page 12)
- any color of construction paper

Directions: Look over each book idea on the "Acorns" worksheet. If the book could be nonfiction, you need to do the following:

1. Cut out the acorn from the worksheet.

2. Cut out a squirrel from "Squirrels" worksheet to go with your acorn.

3. Write the word "nonfiction" on each squirrel you use.

4. Color the squirrel and acorn.

5. On a piece of construction paper, glue the squirrel and nut beside each other.

There are nine squirrels on the "Squirrels" worksheet. You may or may not need all nine squirrels for this activity.

Nuts About Nonfiction

Acorns

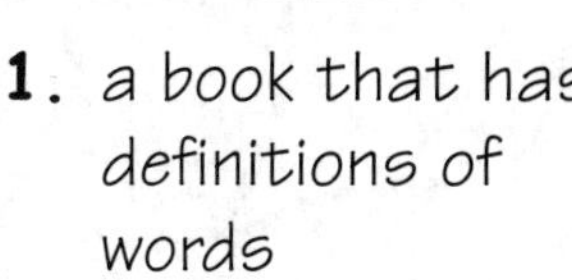

1. a book that has definitions of words

2. a book that has directions for using a computer

3. a book that tells about the Three Little Pigs

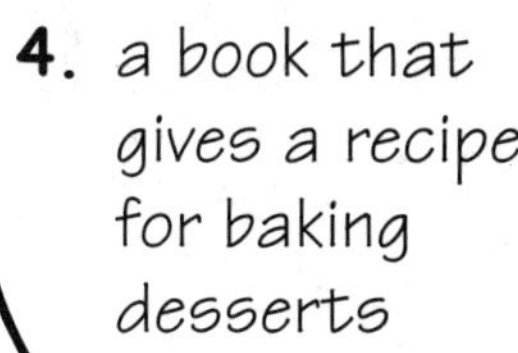

4. a book that gives a recipe for baking desserts

5. a book that a teacher could use in a math class

6. a book that tells about places to visit in Italy

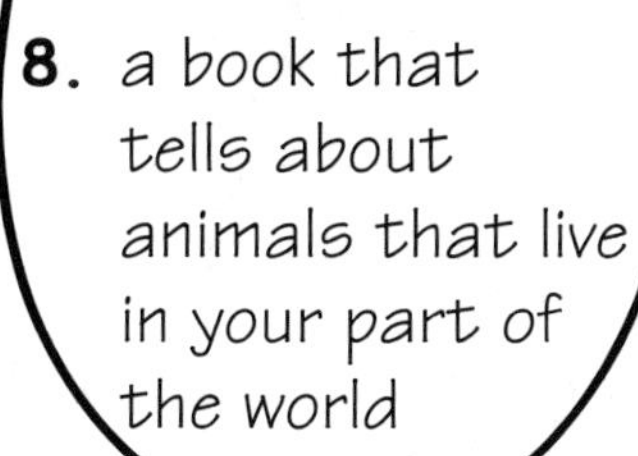

7. a book that tells about two children who travel back in time

8. a book that tells about animals that live in your part of the world

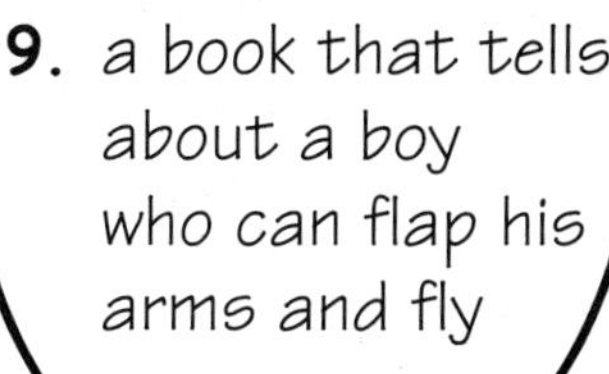

9. a book that tells about a boy who can flap his arms and fly

 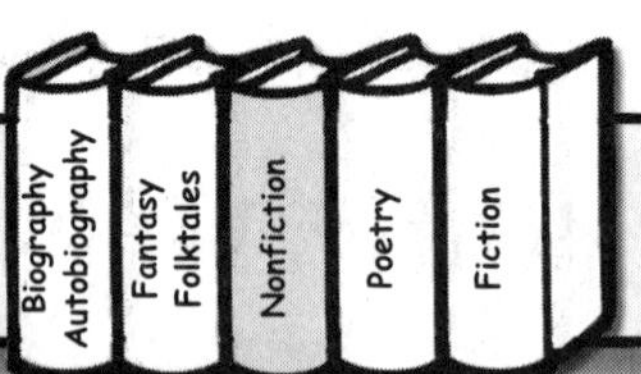

Nuts about Nonfiction

Squirrels

"Bear-ly" There

Nonfiction writing is writing that tells about real people, places, and things. The story being told is not make-believe. Nonfiction gives the reader more information about something that is real.

What if you had to write a report about bears? You may know very little about bears. You would need to use several sources of nonfiction to find out about the topic of your report.

Directions: Look at the picture of each bear. If the information written below it is nonfiction or real, color the bear. If the information is fiction or pretend, write an **X** on the bear.

Bears like to talk to people.	Bears often stand up on their back legs	Polar bears are great swimmers.

Bears love to eat pepperoni pizza.	Bears that live in cold climates spend their winters in a cave or den.	Panda bears mostly eat bamboo, tacos, and hot sauce.

When a bear sleeps through the winter, this sleep is called hibernation.	Most bears like to watch football games on television.	Bears are mammals, and they have an excellent sense of smell.

Yes or No

Nonfiction is writing that has real people, places, and settings. The information in nonfiction writing is true. Nonfiction is writing that gives true information about a topic. Examples of nonfiction would include the textbooks you use at school, the dictionaries or encyclopedias you use for research, and even the directions you read that tell you how to play a game or do some other activity. All of these are examples of nonfiction.

Directions: Read each example. If the example is nonfiction writing, write the word **Yes** on the line. If the example is fiction (not true) writing, write the word **No** on the line.

____________ **1.** the written directions that tell how to play a game

____________ **2.** the writing on the side of a box of brownie mix that explains how to make the brownies

____________ **3.** a book that tells real or factual information about the Pilgrims and the first Thanksgiving

____________ **4.** a book or manual that explains how to play baseball

____________ **5.** a book that tells how to travel back in time

____________ **6.** written directions that explain how to catch a dragon, a fairy, and a unicorn

____________ **7.** a book used in class that teaches how to do science experiments

____________ **8.** the "Z" book from a set of encyclopedias

"Non" Means Not

Nonfiction is writing that is about real people, places, or things. The letters *non* at the front of the word actually mean "not." The word *fiction* means "false" or "pretend." Therefore, *nonfiction* means "not fiction" or "not pretend."

Why do you think certain types of writing would be called nonfiction instead of fiction? What are some reasons a person might need to write nonfiction instead of fiction?

Directions: Look at the pairs of book titles below. Decide which title you think is more likely to be a nonfiction book. Color that book. Put a big **X** over the book that is more likely to be a fiction book.

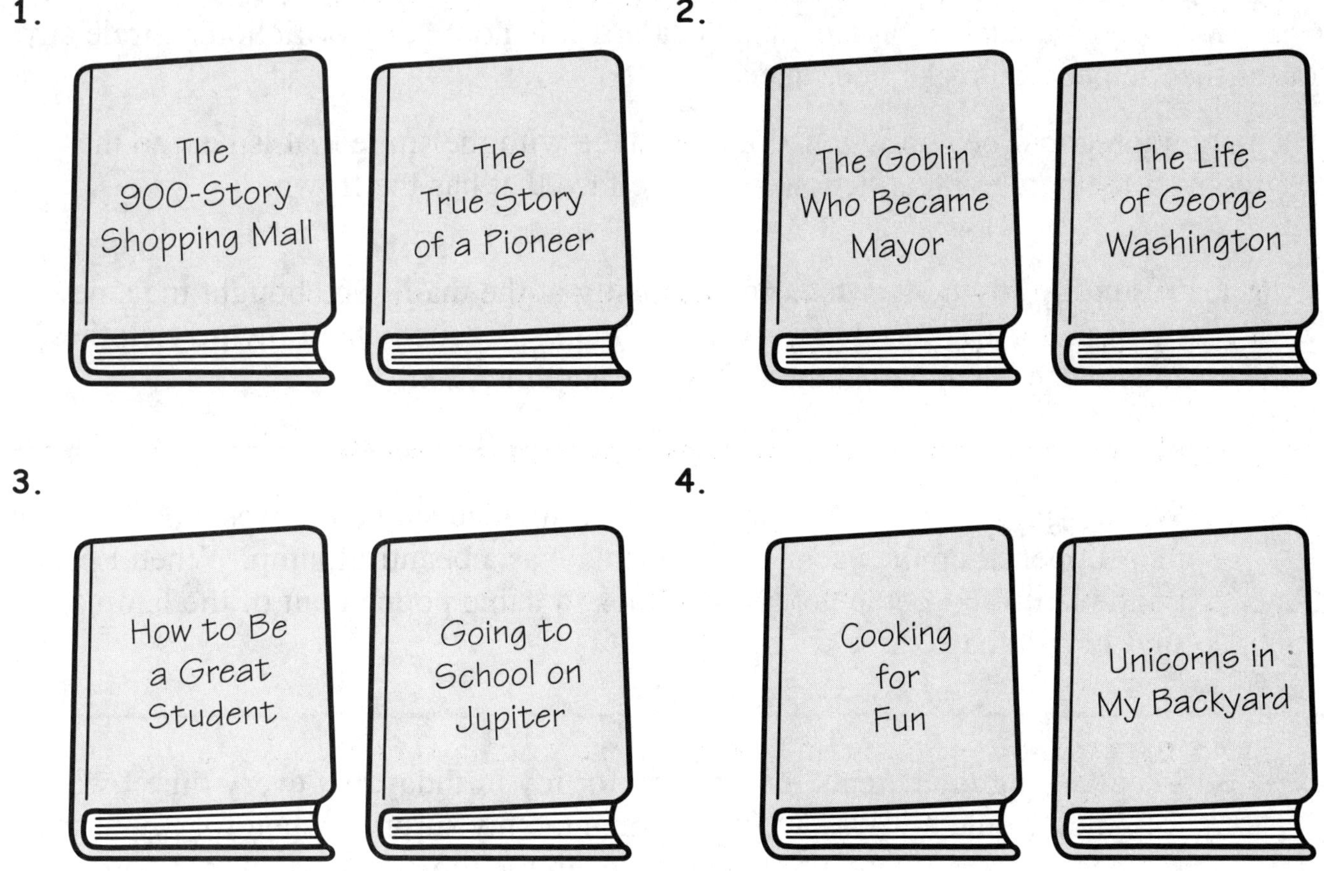

Something Extra: Choose one of the book titles above. Then, on the back of this page, design and color a book cover for the title you have chosen.

Writing About Life

Some people write diaries or journals. When people write about their real lives, they are writing nonfiction. Why? Because the people, places, and things they write about are all true. Nonfiction writing is writing that is all about things that are true.

Have you ever written in a diary or a journal? If so, then you are a nonfiction author!

How can you tell if someone's diary or journal is nonfiction? Well, if he or she lets you read it, you should be able to tell based on what is written. If the events seem possible and true, then the writing is probably nonfiction. But if the writer has written things you know couldn't possibly be true, his or her diary is not really a diary at all but a fiction story. The word *fiction* means that what is written is not true.

Directions: Look at each paragraph and decide if it is nonfiction or fiction. Circle any phrases that helped you make your decision.

If the paragraph could be nonfiction, color the face with the smile that is next to the paragraph. If the paragraph is fiction, color the face that has the frown.

1. Yesterday, my mother took me shopping at the mall. She bought me a new outfit to wear to the spring carnival. I am so excited about my new clothes. I just wish Mom had bought herself something, too!

2. When I got home from school last night, my dad said there was a package for me. I opened up the package and inside was a beautiful lamp. When I picked up the lamp so I could get a better look, a genie popped out of the lamp and said I could have three wishes.

3. I kept asking my parents for a puppy for my birthday, but every time I would ask, they would always say, "No." Imagine my surprise when for my birthday my parents carried out a box with holes in the top and a bright, red bow. I hurried to open the box, and there inside was the cutest puppy I had ever seen! Imagine my surprise when my puppy opened its mouth and said "Hello" to me.

Learning Nonfiction

Directions: Answer each question.

1. Use a dictionary to look up the definition for *nonfiction*. Write it here.

   ____

   ____

2. If you could read a nonfiction book about one topic, what topic would you choose? Why would you choose this topic?____

   ____

3. Books about hobbies are nonfiction books. Would you rather read a book about coin collecting, stamp collecting, or card collecting? Why?

   ____

   ____

4. Some nonfiction books are updated each year. Why do you think a nonfiction book might need to be rewritten or have information added to it each year?

   ____

   ____

5. In the library, nonfiction books are identified by looking at the spine of the book. On the spine will be two letters: *NF.* What do you think these letters stand for?

   ____

6. Why do you think someone would enjoy reading nonfiction?___________________________

   ____

What Is What?

Nonfiction is writing that is true or real. Fiction writing is writing that is not true or real.
There are many, many different types of nonfiction. When you get up to eat your cereal
for breakfast, there is writing on the cereal box. That is nonfiction—but that is only one
type of nonfiction writing.

Nonfiction writing can include things such as textbooks, directions, brochures, letters,
diaries, newspapers, and magazines.

Directions: Draw a line and match each word to its description.

1. nonfiction

2. fiction

3. characters

4. setting

5. plot

6. textbooks

7. directions

8. diary

a. books written about school subjects

b. people or animals that the story is
   written about

c. writing that is not real or true

d. writing that explains how to do
   something

e. writing that is true or real

f. where and when a story takes place
   or happens

g. personal writings about someone's
   daily life

h. the action of a story; what happens

Learn It!

Nonfiction writing is writing that is about real people, places, or things. Nonfiction writing usually teaches the reader something new. There are certain types of writing that can be easily be defined as nonfiction writing. Follow the directions below to see how much you know about these special words.

Directions: Use what you already know or use the library to help you define and explain the following types of nonfiction writing.

1. textbooks ________________________________

____

2. directions ________________________________

____

3. autobiographies ________________________________

____

4. biographies ________________________________

____

5. diaries ________________________________

____

6. reference books ________________________________

____

7. newspapers ________________________________

____

8. magazines ________________________________

____

Looking at the Word

Nonfiction means writing that is real or true. *Non* is a prefix that means "not." So, nonfiction writing is writing that is not fiction. Well, what is fiction? Fiction is writing that is not real or true. Fiction writing is filled with make-believe or imaginary events.

Many words have extra prefixes added onto them to change the meaning of the word. A *prefix* is a part that is added to the front of a word. We add the prefix *non* to the word *fiction* to make a new word: *nonfiction*.

Part I

Directions: Add the prefix *non* to the words below to create new words. Write the new words on the line. Don't forget, the prefix *non* means "no" or "not."

1. non   +   sense   = _______________________________________

2. non   +   fat   = _______________________________________

3. non   +   stop   = _______________________________________

4. non   +   stick   = _______________________________________

5. non   +   dairy   = _______________________________________

Part II

Directions: Choose any three of your five new words from Part I and use them in your own sentences. Write your sentences on the lines below.

1. _______________________________________

____

2. _______________________________________

____

3. _______________________________________

____

Word Help Is Here!

Sometimes you may have trouble telling if what you are reading is nonfiction or fiction. Never fear! There is help out there for anyone who needs it. When you read, you can look for vocabulary clues that can help you while you are reading. Also, there are some familiar story beginnings that are most often used with fictional stories.

Directions: Look at the story starters below. Decide if what is written would help you know if you are reading fiction or nonfiction.

- Color the rectangle *red* if the starters more likely go with fiction writing.

- Color the rectangle *yellow* if the starters more likely go with nonfiction writing.

Learning New Vocabulary

It is always exciting to learn something new. Learning new words can also be fun. One way to learn some new words is to look through an encyclopedia. An encyclopedia is one type of nonfiction writing. Encyclopedias are updated each year so that the information inside them stays current. Encyclopedias are arranged alphabetically so that the information is easy to find. If you could read through a set of encyclopedias from A through Z, you would definitely learn a lot of new words!

Directions: With the help of your teacher or librarian, find a set of encyclopedias either in the library or on the computer.

✎ *Now, write your first name here:* _______________________________

Next, look at your first name. Circle the first letter.

Now, get the encyclopedia that starts with the letter you have circled. Look up five words from the encyclopedia.

Write down the five words, and then write down what you think each word means. Use each encyclopedia entry to help you understand each word.

1. New Word: ____

  Definition: ____

2. New Word: ____

  Definition: ____

3. New Word: ____

  Definition: ____

4. New Word: ____

  Definition: ____

5. New Word: ____

  Definition: ____

Sack Full of Facts

Nonfiction books are filled with facts. To understand a nonfiction book, you need to know what a fact is. A fact is something that can be proven to be true.

Examples: February is the shortest month of the year. (*This is a fact. February has fewer days than any other month. This can be proven, and so it is a fact.*)

February is the best month of the year. (*This is not a fact. It cannot be proven. Some people may love February, but some people may not.*)

Directions: Each sack below has a topic written underneath it. Fill the sack with as many facts as you know about each topic. You can write your facts as notes; in other words, you do not have to write in complete sentences.

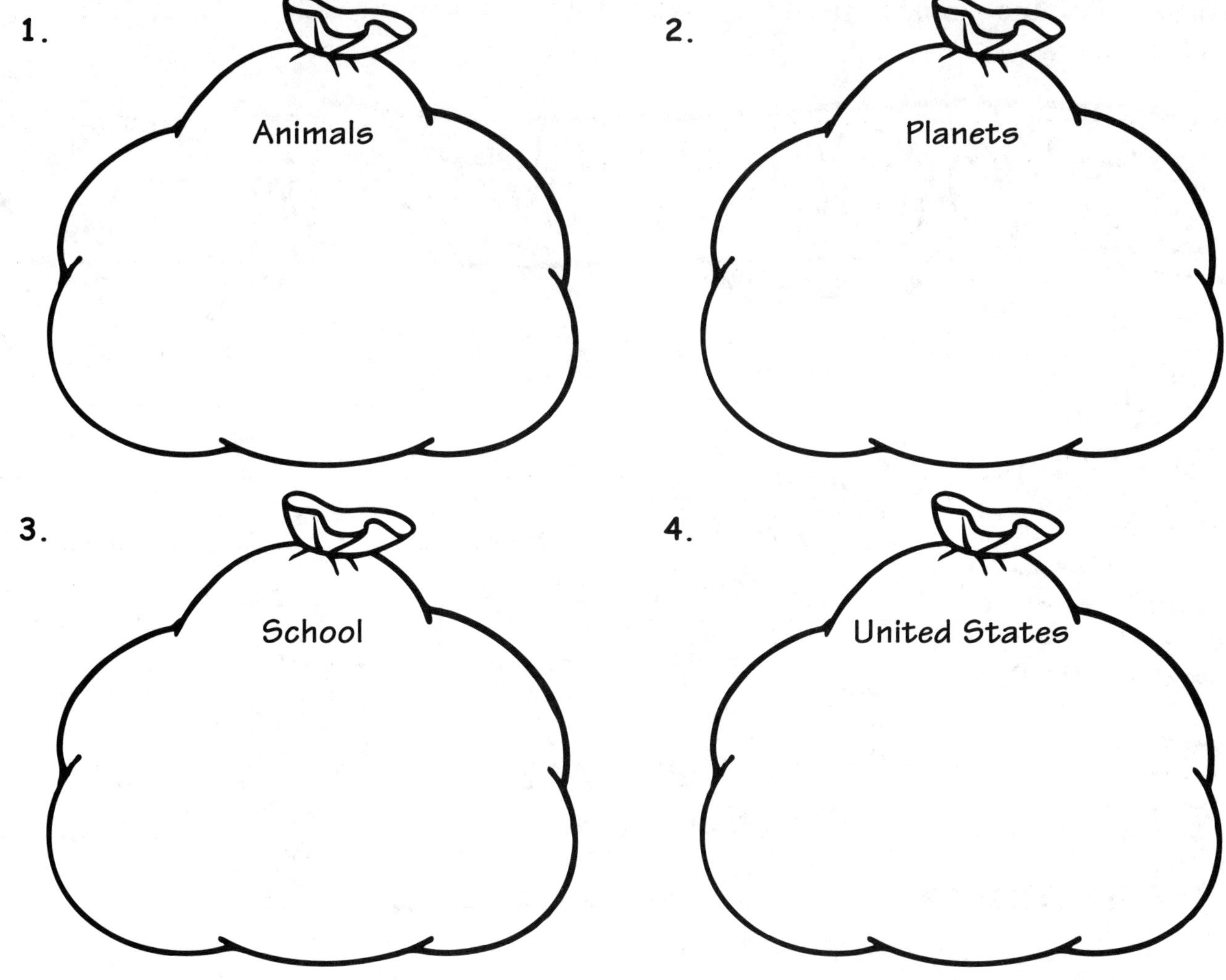

Newspaper Vocabulary

Newspapers are a popular form of nonfiction writing. Newspapers have a unique set of vocabulary words you need to understand if you want to be a good newspaper writer.

Directions: Look at the large newspaper below. Each section has an arrow pointing to it. Here are the four sections:

| 1. picture | 2. masthead | 3. headline | 4. caption |

In the circle connected to each arrow, write the number of the section the arrow is pointing to. Use the numbers from the box above.

Reading the Story

Nonfiction writing is writing that is filled with facts. The information you read in nonfiction writing is true. But that doesn't mean the writing is boring; it is just the opposite. Nonfiction writing can be filled with fascinating information.

Directions: Read the following nonfiction story. Answer the questions that follow.

The Great Wall of China

Look at a wall in your classroom. How long do you think it is? Now think about the Great Wall of China. This wall is 1,500 miles (2,414 km) long! It averages about 25 feet (7.6 m) in height. Some people even say that the Great Wall of China is the only man-made thing on Earth that can be seen from outer space!

So why was this wall built? Well, many, many years ago it was thought that this wall would help protect China's border. The emperor, or ruler, thought the wall would stop his enemies from crossing into China.

1. How long is the Great Wall of China? _______________________________________

2. Why do you think the Great Wall of China could be seen from outer space?

____

____

3. Why was the wall built? _______________________________________

____

4. Do you think the wall helped keep out China's enemies? Why or why not?

____

____

Real Stories

Nonfiction stories are often exciting to read because they are filled with real information. It is fun to be able to read something and think, "Wow! That really happened."

Directions: Read the nonfiction story and complete the activity below.

Going Over the Falls

Niagara Falls is a famous waterfall on the border between the United States and Canada. When Annie Taylor was 63 years old, she decided to go over Niagara Falls in a barrel! One woman had tried before Taylor, but she had not survived. To help her survive, Taylor designed a special barrel. It was so small she had to wiggle her way into the barrel, but it had iron hoops in it for strength. The barrel weighed 160 lbs!

Taylor survived going over the falls. She had lots of bruises and a slight concussion. When it was over, Taylor said, "It was a terrible nightmare, and I'd sooner be shot by a cannon…than do it again." Taylor was famous for a short time, but she died penniless.

Directions: Below is a picture of a barrel. Draw you with your head showing at the top of the barrel. Then beside the barrel list five things you would be scared to do.

1. _______________________________

2. _______________________________

3. _______________________________

4. _______________________________

5. _______________________________

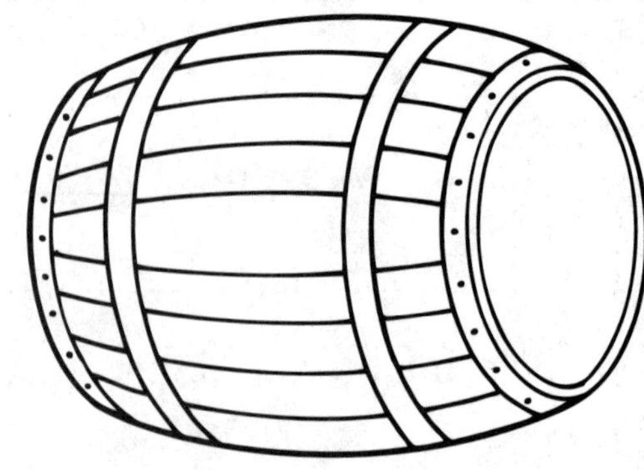

Why do you think Annie Taylor decided to go over Niagara Falls?

Reading Directions

Directions are a type of nonfiction writing. You may read directions on how to put together a toy or on how to get somewhere. Knowing how to read directions is an important skill. When you are reading directions, you should be sure to read all the directions first. Also, you should follow the directions in the order the steps are written.

Directions: For this activity, wait for your teacher to tell you when to begin. You are to do this entire activity with no help from your teacher. Read each sentence below before you begin working. Be sure to follow all the directions you are given.

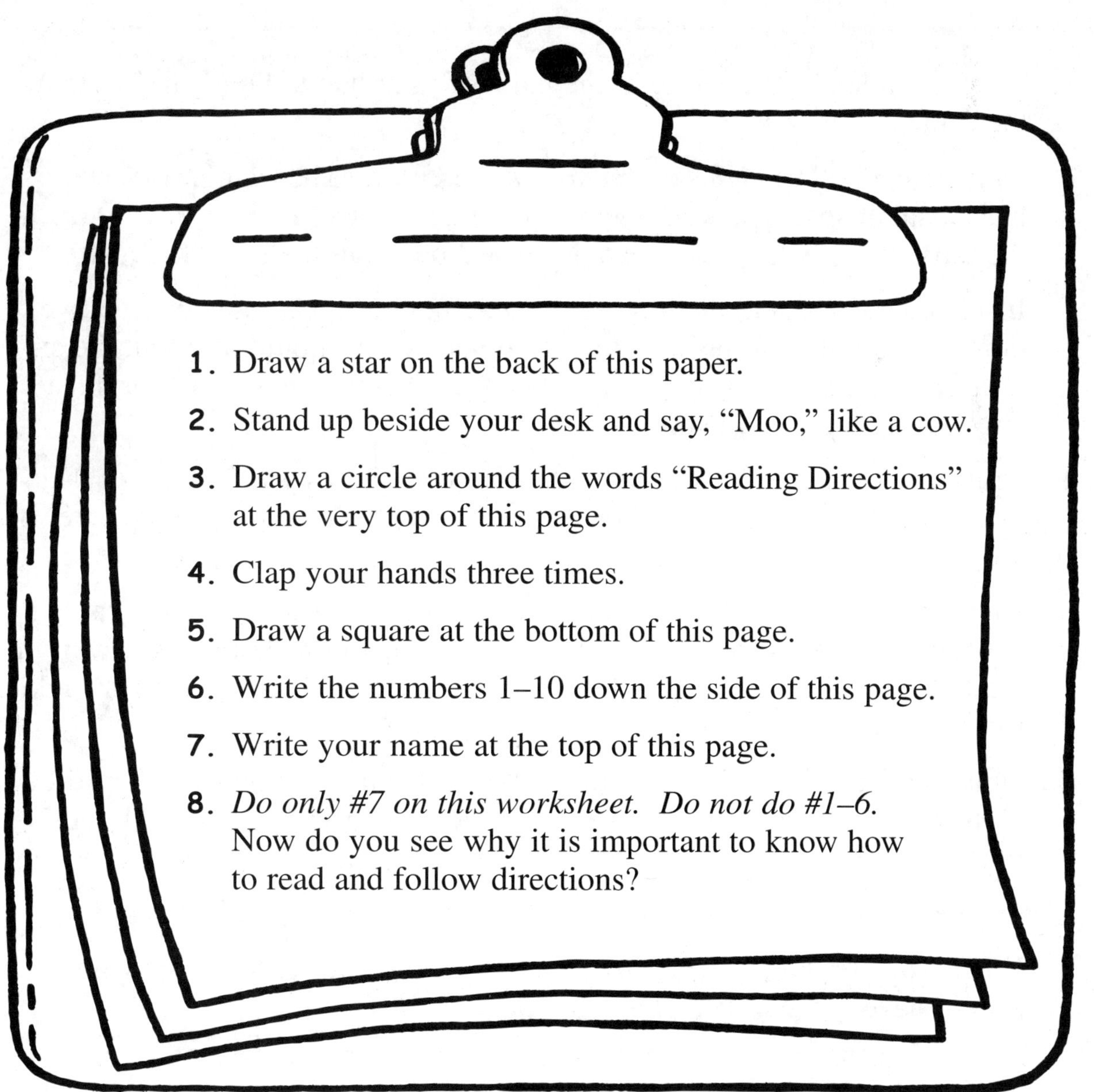

1. Draw a star on the back of this paper.

2. Stand up beside your desk and say, "Moo," like a cow.

3. Draw a circle around the words "Reading Directions" at the very top of this page.

4. Clap your hands three times.

5. Draw a square at the bottom of this page.

6. Write the numbers 1–10 down the side of this page.

7. Write your name at the top of this page.

8. *Do only #7 on this worksheet. Do not do #1–6.*
   Now do you see why it is important to know how to read and follow directions?

How You Do It

Directions are not exciting to read, but they are a very important type of nonfiction writing because they let you know how to do something.

When you read directions, you need to read each step. Do not leave out any of the steps, because each one is important.

Directions: Read the directions below. See if you can follow them exactly as they are given. Use your own paper to draw a picture using the directions given.

1. Draw a circle about the size of the palm of your hand. Draw the circle in the center of your paper.

2. Draw two small triangles on the top of the circle. The triangles should have a small space between them. The base of each triangle should touch the top of the circle. Each triangle should be about the size of a quarter.

3. Inside the circle, near the top of the circle but not touching the top curve, draw two smaller circles next to each other. They should be about the size of dimes. Be sure to leave a space between the two circles. Color in each circle using a green crayon.

4. Draw one circle just underneath the other two circles you just drew. This circle should be slightly smaller than a dime and should be in the center of the original circle.

5. Draw six short lines. Three of the lines should be drawn off the right edge of the circle you just drew. The remaining three lines should be drawn off the left side of the circle. Each line should be about as long as your pinkie finger.

6. Draw one last circle. This circle goes underneath the circle you first drew. It should be the same size as the last circle you drew, but it should not touch the other circle. Color this circle pink or red.

7. On the line below the picture, write the name of what you have drawn.

8. When you are finished, ask the teacher to show you what the drawing should have looked like. How did you do?

Directions with Abbreviations

One type of nonfiction reading is reading directions. Sometimes directions are written using abbreviations.

Part I

Directions: Look at each abbreviation that is commonly used in writing directions, and see if you can write the word for the abbreviation.

1. ave. _______________________________

2. st. _______________________________

3. rt. _______________________________

4. dr. _______________________________

5. rd. _______________________________

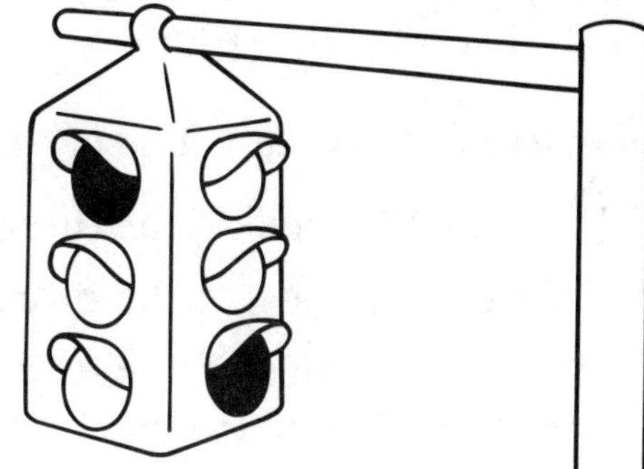

Part II

Directions: Look at the common direction words written in the box below. Use at least three of them to write three sentences of your own. **Helpful Hint:** Remember to capitalize the direction word if it begins a sentence or is used in a specific address.

north	south	up	down	west	east
street	road	drive	place	route	avenue

1. ____

____

2. ____

____

3. ____

____

More Reading Directions

Directions are a type of nonfiction writing. Reading directions is an important skill to learn. You may need to read directions on an assignment at school. You may need to read directions on how to get to a friend's house. You may need to read directions to know how to build a toy. You use this skill each and every day.

When you are reading directions, pay special attention to the order of the directions. Look for key words such as *first, next,* or *later*. These transition words help you know the order of the directions.

Directions: Look at each set of mixed-up directions written below.

- ✐ Write a "**1**" beside the direction that should go first.
- ✐ Write a "**2**" beside the direction that should go second.
- ✐ Write a "**3**" beside the direction that should go third.

1.

_____ **a.** Finally, place the candles on the top.

_____ **b.** You will first buy a cake and candles.

_____ **c.** Take the cake and candles out of their boxes.

2.

_____ **a.** First, blow up the balloon.

_____ **b.** When you have tied the balloon, add a string or streamer.

_____ **c.** Tie the balloon at the bottom so that no air will escape.

3.

_____ **a.** The second thing to do is pick out the toy you want.

_____ **b.** First, see if you can get permission to go to the store.

_____ **c.** The third step is to find the toy and buy it.

4.

_____ **a.** Next, see if the water is warm enough for you.

_____ **b.** You want to swim in the pool, but you need to check the water.

_____ **c.** Finally, if it is warm, go ahead and jump in!

Putting It In Order

Directions must be written in correct order for them to be helpful. See what you can do about placing the directions below in the correct order.

Directions: Read and cut out each sentence strip. Then, on another piece of paper, glue the strips in the order they should go.

Brushing Your Teeth

Rinse your mouth of toothpaste.

Get your toothbrush.

Brush your teeth.

Just before you rinse, fill your rinsing cup with water.

Put toothpaste on your toothbrush.

Following Directions

Reading directions is an important nonfiction reading skill. Nonfiction is writing that is about real things. You definitely would not ever want to have made-up directions! What if you were trying to cook a recipe and the cook had simply made something up?

Directions: Read and follow the directions below. See if they are made-up or real.

Drawing 1: House

1. Draw a square in the space to the right.

2. On top of the square, draw a triangle. The base of the triangle should be the same length as the top of the square.

3. Draw a small rectangle up from the bottom of the square. This rectangle is the door for your house.

4. Draw two small squares inside the big square. Draw one on the right and one on the left. These are the windows.

5. Color your house.

   Did you draw a house? ____________

   Were these directions real or made-up? ____

Drawing 2: Cat

1. Draw a circle in the space to the right.

2. Draw a triangle inside the circle.

3. Draw two eyes inside the triangle.

4. Draw a square around the first circle.

5. Color your cat.

   Did you draw a cat? ____________

   Were the directions real or made-up? ____

School's Out

Nonfiction books are often loaded with pictures. These pictures go with the text or writing that is in the book. The pictures help the reader better understand what each section is about. The pictures also help prove the truth of the words.

Directions: Look at the picture below. Write a nonfiction description to tell what is happening in the picture. Then color the picture.

____

____

____

____

____

____

Something Extra: On the back of this page, draw a picture that might be found in a social studies textbook. See if a friend can guess the truth about your drawing.

Reading Special Features

Textbooks are a type of nonfiction writing. Many textbooks share similar features. Most have a table of contents, a glossary, and an index.

- The **table of contents** is the outline of everything that will be found in the book. It gives page numbers and titles for each section. The table of contents can be found at the front of the textbook.
- The **glossary** is a specialized dictionary. It is organized alphabetically but only contains words that can be found in the textbook. The glossary gives a definition for each of the words listed.
- The **index** is also listed alphabetically. The index gives page numbers where information can be found about any item that is listed.

  The glossary and index are both in the back of a textbook.

Directions: Write the correct answer.

1. Textbooks are an example of what type of writing? _______________________

2. Where might you use a textbook? _______________________

3. What are three important sections of most textbooks? _______________________

____

4. Which of the three sections can be found at the front of the textbook?

____

5. Which two of the three sections can be found at the back of the textbook?

____

6. Which two of these sections are organized alphabetically?

____

7. If you needed a definition for a word in the book, which section would you check?

____

8. Look at a textbook you have in your classroom. Turn to the table of contents. Write the title and page number of the first piece of information that is given there.

____

Reading the Text

When you started school, you probably saw your very first textbook. Textbooks are filled with true information about a particular subject in school. They are made for all types of school subjects, including English, math, science, and social studies. Textbooks usually organize information by chapters. The front of the textbook will have a table of contents to help you find information. Most textbooks also have a glossary to help define words found in the book and an index to help you find page numbers for topics listed in the book.

Directions: Below are different pages in a textbook. Answer each question based on the information given.

Table of Contents

Parts of Speech 8

Writing a Narrative. . . . 34

Capitalization. 42

Punctuation. 77

Glossary 88

Glossary

adjective—a word that describes nouns or pronouns

noun—a word that names a person, place, thing, or idea

pronoun—a word that takes the place of a noun

1. What type of textbook do you think the table of contents and glossary belong to?

____

2. According to the table of contents, what can be found on page 88 of this book?

____

3. According to the glossary, what is a pronoun?

____

4. Looking at the glossary page, how do you think the words in this glossary are arranged?

____

Reference Nonfiction

An important type of nonfiction writing is reference books. Reference books are materials you can use to find information about certain topics. There are many types of reference books; some examples are encyclopedias, atlases, and almanacs.

- ✎ **Encyclopedias** are organized alphabetically by topic. Each book usually covers one or two letters of the alphabet.
- ✎ **Atlases** usually include maps and information about particular areas of the world.
- ✎ **Almanacs** are filled with important facts about a general topic. For example, the almanac farmers use is filled with important information that is relevant to farmers. This almanac might tell a farmer what the best month is to plant corn, beans, or other crops.

Reference books are nonfiction and are usually found in a special section in the library. Many libraries do not allow reference books to be checked out of the library. These books stay so that people who need to do research can easily find what they are looking for.

Directions: Look at the book titles. Color only the books that might be reference books.

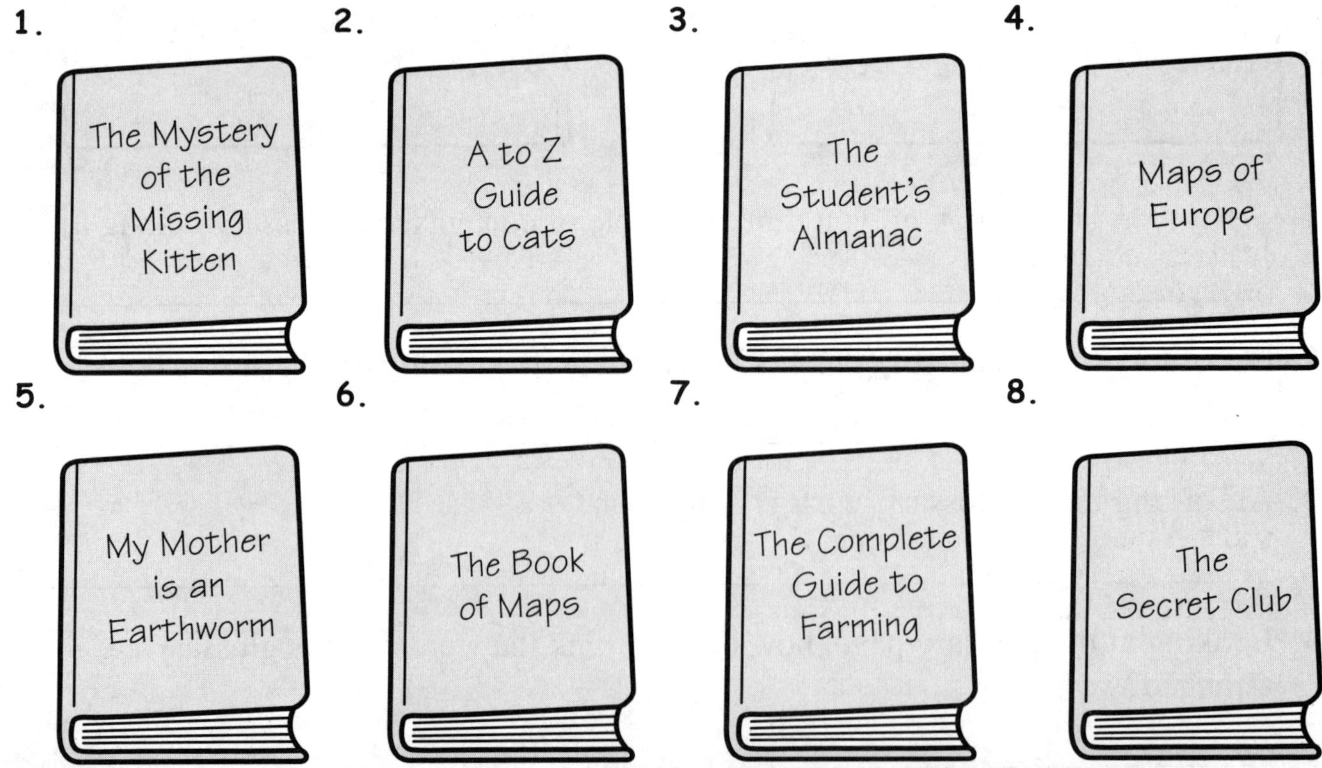

Reading for Information

Reference books are a type of nonfiction writing. Reference nonfiction is writing that is filled with information about a particular topic. Encyclopedias are one of the most common types of reference book. Encyclopedias are organized alphabetically. For example, if you want to look up information about aardvarks, you would go to the "A" encyclopedia and then look for the word in the book. The words inside each book are also organized alphabetically. In what part of the "A" encyclopedia do you think the word *aardvark* would be found? Would it be in the front, the middle, or the back of the book?

Directions: Answer each question.

1. List three topics you might find in the "M" encyclopedia.

_________________   _________________   _________________

2. Would information you find in an encyclopedia be fiction or nonfiction?

____

3. How are encyclopedias organized?

____

4. If you wanted to find out information about Abraham Lincoln, which encyclopedia would you use?

____

5. With the help of your teacher or librarian, find an encyclopedia that starts with the same letter as your last name.

What is the first entry listed in the encyclopedia? _________________________

What is the last entry listed in the encyclopedia? _________________________

The Great Race

Reference books are an important type of nonfiction. If you wanted to know the year man first landed on the moon, you could go to a reference book to find that information. One of the best reference sources that could be used to find this same information is the Internet. It is quick and easy, and most people can find a way to use the Internet even if it is not available at home. Many public libraries offer Internet service for free.

Before using reference information from the Internet, the user needs to make sure the source is reliable. Books are often checked by editors for accuracy and truth, but the Internet is not like this. People can write almost anything; it is up to the reader to decide if the information is true. Children should never use the Internet—even if looking for information—without permission from an adult.

Some computers have their own electronic encyclopedias. These are also a great source for reference materials.

Directions: With your teacher's help, find a partner. Race against the other groups in the class to find the answers to the questions below. You may use any reference source.

1. Who was the second president of the United States of America?

   ____

2. List the names of the seven continents.

   _________________   _________________   _________________   _________________

   _________________   _________________   _________________

3. What is the capital city of the state of Georgia? _______________________________

4. What are the seven colors in a rainbow?

   _________________   _________________   _________________   _________________

   _________________   _________________   _________________

5. What two countries border, or touch, the United States?

   ___________________________________   ___________________________________

Read It

Directions: Read the following reference material and then answer the questions.

Tortoises and Turtles

Tortoises and turtles are ancient animals that first appeared on Earth more than 200 million years ago, when the dinosaurs were alive. Their appearance has changed very little in all this time. They are easy to recognize because they have heavy shells covering their backs. Tortoises are land animals, but turtles spend most of their life either in or by water. Both turtles and tortoises belong to a group of animals called reptiles, which have scaly skin and lay leathery eggs.

1. Would the above paragraph most likely be found in a fiction book or a nonfiction book? Explain your answer. ___________________________

   ____

2. List three facts about turtles and tortoises: ___________________________

   ____

3. Why are turtles and tortoises easy to recognize?

   ____

4. What group of animals do tortoises and turtles belong to?

   ____

5. When did turtles and tortoises first appear on Earth?

   ____

6. If you wanted to look up more information about turtles or tortoises, in which encyclopedia would you look? ___________________________

Something Extra: On the back of this paper, draw a picture of you swimming with a turtle. When you are finished with your drawing, be sure to color your picture.

Stay Out!

Have you ever kept a diary? Most people do at some point. Maybe they write one at home, or maybe their teacher assigns them a journal-writing activity each day. Whatever is written, most people keep their diary entries private; this means that they do not want to share what they have written.

Diaries and journals are examples of nonfiction writing. In most cases, the writer is not writing a fiction story; instead, the writer is documenting or writing about certain moments or events that happened in his or her life.

Directions: Read the diary entry and answer the questions.

March 28,

Today is a terrible day. It is raining outside, so I will not get to have soccer practice. I forgot my umbrella, so when I walk home from school I am going to get soaking wet. When I went to lunch and opened my lunch box, I had the worst lunch ever: a jelly sandwich. My bread was soggy, and I missed the peanut butter. I can't wait for tomorrow to get here so I can have a new day!

1. Do you think the writer of this entry is happy or sad? Explain your answer.

____

2. What type of day did the writer say he or she was having?

____

____

3. List two things that made the day this way.

____

____

____

4. Have you ever had a really great day? Explain why that day was so great.

____

5. If you wrote in a diary, would you write in it every day? Why or why not?

____

Daily Diary

One type of nonfiction writing that is very popular is writing in a diary. Nonfiction writing is writing that is true or not fiction. When someone writes about his life, he is writing about true events that occurred to him.

When people are famous, their journals or diaries will sometimes become books. These nonfiction writings are wonderful because they give the reader lots of information about what a person was thinking or how he really felt about a certain topic.

Directions: Imagine a diary has been found for each person listed below. Imagine each of the diaries is going to be published as books. Write a good title for each possible book.

Person Who Wrote the Diary	Book Title
1. George Washington	
2. Abraham Lincoln	
3. Pocahontas	
4. Martin Luther King, Jr.	
5. a Pilgrim at the first Thanksgiving	

Now, imagine your own diary is going to be published into a book for others to read. What title would you want to give your diary? Write your title on the book to the right.

Historical Documents

Directions: Read the article about historical documents and then answer the questions below.

Historical documents are a type of nonfiction writing. Historical documents are important writings from the past. There are many famous historical documents. One historical document is the Mayflower Compact. This document was written by the Pilgrims when they came to the New World. The Pilgrims were a group of people from England who were trying to reach North America. They were originally headed for the Jamestown colony, but they did not arrive at Jamestown; instead, they landed at Plymouth Rock.

Before the Pilgrims began their new colony, they knew they would need a set of rules. The Mayflower Compact was their set of rules to help make the colony successful. They named the document after the ship on which they had sailed, the Mayflower. Can you think of some rules that might have helped the colonists be successful?

1. What is a historical document?

____

2. What group of people wrote the Mayflower Compact?

____

3. What was the name of the Pilgrim's ship?

____

4. What was the Mayflower Compact?

____

5. Why do you think it was important for the Pilgrims to have written rules?

____

6. What are some rules you have to follow at home or at school?

____

History Has It

Historical writing is very important. In fact, much of what we know about history comes from the many historical writings that were recorded and passed down from generation to generation.

Some documents are so important that they have helped to rule nations. In the United States, there are three very important historical documents. These documents are the Declaration of Independence, the Bill of Rights, and the Constitution. The Declaration of Independence is important because this was the document the original 13 colonies agreed upon when declaring their independence from England. The Bill of Rights lists the rights they believed all people should have, such as freedom of expression. Finally, the Constitution is important because it describes how the United States would be governed. These three documents are so important that without them there might not be a United States of America.

Directions: Draw a line to match each set.

1. **The Declaration of Independence**

2. **The Constitution**

3. **The Bill of Rights**

4. **historical nonfiction**

5. **historical fiction**

A. writing that is about true or real events in history

B. a document listing the rights of the people

C. a historical document written by the 13 colonies to England, declaring independence

D. the written laws and rules governing the United States

E. writing that is not true but is based on a true or real event

How to Read a Newspaper

Newspapers are a popular form of nonfiction writing. They are filled with true stories written by newspaper reporters. These reporters are often taught to write by using the five *Ws*: *who, what, when, where,* and *why*. If a reporter answers all of these questions in his article, he will have everything the reader needs for a good piece of nonfiction.

Newspapers have headlines for each article, and many articles also have pictures. The headlines capture the reader's attention, so that he'll know if he wants to read more. The pictures give images to go with the story.

Because newspapers are not usually expensive and are easy to get, they are one of the most popular forms of nonfiction. Most newspapers can also be found on-line for people who do not want to have a newspaper delivered to their home.

Directions: Read the following newspaper article. Then identify the *Ws*.

Man Dognaps Pet

Miami, Florida—A man from Florida stole his neighbor's dog on Friday, August 28. Mr. Arthur Townes and his neighbor, Mr. Eric Jones, were having an argument about a dog named Scooter. Townes wanted Scooter, but Jones was Scooter's owner and did not want to give his dog to Townes. This is when Townes apparently decided to dognap the little pooch. Driving an old pickup truck, Townes made it all the way to Texas before the police were able to stop him. When questioned about why he took the dog, Townes was quoted as saying that Scooter was "a doggone good dog." Mr. Townes has been taken back to Florida, where he will have to wait to hear from a judge regarding this unusual case of dognapping.

1. *Who* is this story about? ____

2. *What* is this story about?____

3. *When* did this story take place? ____

4. *Where* did this story take place?____

5. *Why* did this happen? ____

In the News

Newspapers are a very popular form of nonfiction. Newspapers are filled with current information. If you don't want to, you do not have to read the entire paper; you can skip around and read only the parts that interest you.

Newspapers are often divided into sections. There are sections such as "Local News" and "World News." Some sections even have local advertisements and a list of things that are for sale. The newspaper also has a few sections that are not nonfiction, like the comics.

Directions: Read the newspaper article. Answer the questions that follow.

Girl Saves Cat

Carmel, Kentucky—Kaycee Lynn, a 10-year-old girl from Carmel, was a hero on the Fourth of July when she saved a cat from drowning. Sparkle, a calico cat that belongs to Lynn's neighbor, lost its balance and fell into a small pond. The cat was unable to get out because the sides of the pond were too slick. Seeing the cat in distress, the young girl acted quickly. She held out a tree branch for the cat to jump on and then helped the cat get to safety. Sparkle's owner, Mrs. Emilee Watson, claims Kaycee was a true hero.

1. What is the headline of the article? _______________________________________

2. Who saved the cat? ____

3. Why did the cat need saving? ____

   ____

4. How did the young girl save the cat?

   ____

5. Do you think the young girl was really a hero? Why or why not?

   ____

6. What do you think makes someone a hero?

   ____

Reading a Magazine

Most magazines are generally made of nonfiction articles. They also contain several pictures and are usually printed in color. Also, a magazine will usually appeal to (be liked by) a certain group. For example, a magazine called *Great Dogs* would probably only interest people who love dogs.

Directions: Look at the magazine cover to the right. Then answer each question.

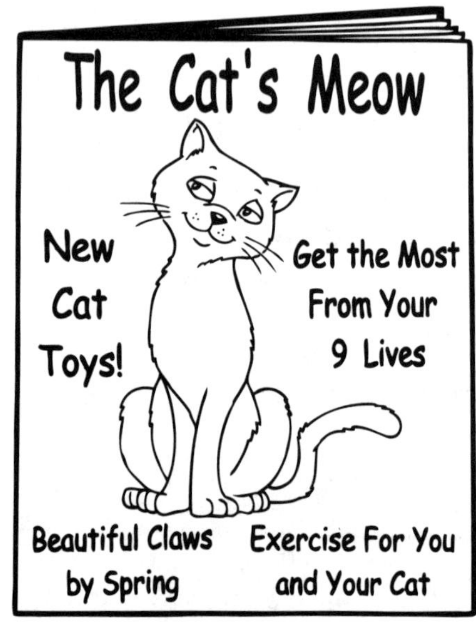

1. What is the name of the magazine?

   ____

2. Who do you think would like to read this type of magazine?

   ____

3. Who do you think would not like to read this type of magazine?

   ____

4. List two stories you can find inside this issue:

   ____

   ____

5. Write an article headline that could appear in this magazine.

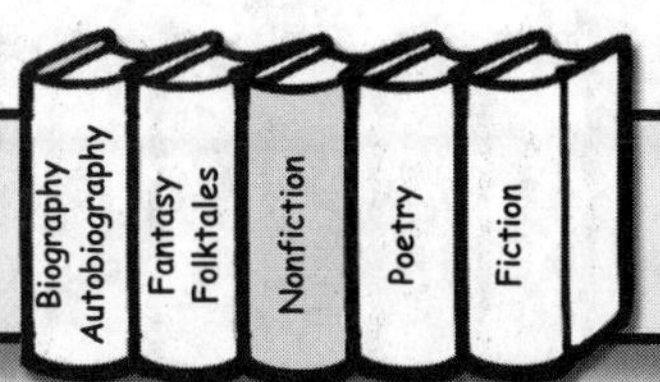

Everywhere There Are Signs

Signs and labels are everywhere. Most of these are nonfiction writing. These signs and labels are there for many important reasons. Sometimes there might be wet paint—and a sign saying "Wet Paint" can keep someone from making a mess.

Can you think of some other important signs that might be a help to people?

Directions: Look at the signs below and their symbols. Write what each sign means.

1.	**2.**	**3.**
4.	**5.**	**6.**

Something Extra: Can you think of any other signs? Draw your signs on a separate piece of paper and see if a friend can guess what each one means.

Looking for Clues

Do you like to learn new things? If you do, you should enjoy reading nonfiction.
Brochures are a form of nonfiction writing. "Brochure" looks like it might be a hard
word to say. Try to remember it like this: the first syllable of the word is pronounced
"bro," like a nickname for the word "brother." The second part of the word sounds like
"sure." Now try it again: *brochure*.

Okay, now that you know how to say the word, what is a brochure? A brochure is a
pamphlet filled with information about a topic. The topic is usually nonfiction but
sometimes it can be fiction. If you were on a vacation and you wanted information
about certain places to visit, you might pick up and read some brochures about where
you want to go. Some people write brochures to explain a certain product. Some people
write brochures to tell about their businesses. There are many reasons to write and read
brochures.

Part I

Directions: Look at the brochure or pamphlet below. Then go to Part II on page 49.

Best Pet Ever!

Have you ever wanted a pet but didn't know what to get? The best pet is something you can find right in your own home: a DUST BUNNY! It needs no food or water. It's soft and cuddly, and it's free!

You Need One of These

You'll be able to convince your parents to get you a dust bunny because it doesn't cost them any money, and you will be cleaning up the house instead of getting it dirty! Does your mom ever complain about the dust in your room? Now you can turn that dust into the pet you've always wanted.

Fun! Fun! Fun!

What could be more fun than you and your new dust bunny hanging out at home together?

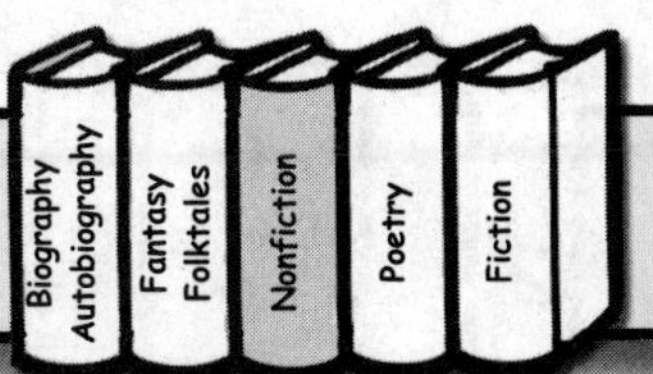

Looking for Clues

Part II

Directions: Use the brochure on page 48 to answer the questions below.

1. What is this pamphlet advertising?

____

____

2. Is the information in this pamphlet fiction or nonfiction?

____

____

3. How do you know?

____

____

4. Can you think of any places where you might find a brochure?

____

____

Part III

Directions: Now it is your turn to make a brochure. Fold a piece of paper into three even sections.

Now design a brochure advertising a real place that you have been. Remember to include facts about the place you chose. Also add pictures to make your brochure something everyone will want to pick up and read.

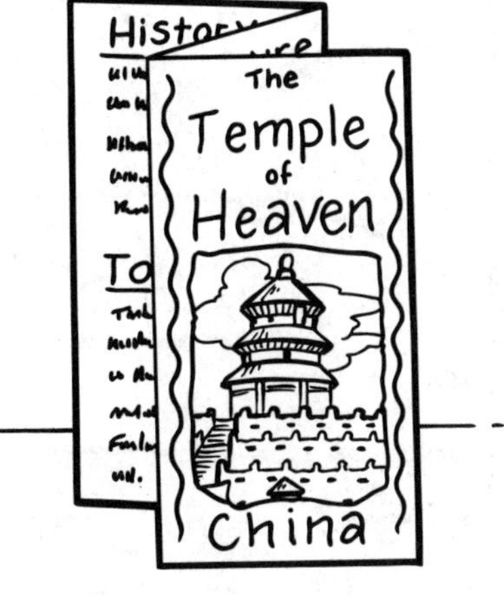

Biographies

George Washington. Abraham Lincoln. Martin Luther King, Jr. What do all of these people have in common? They all have biographies written about them. What is a biography? A biography is a book about someone's life. A biography is about one person but written by another person. You might wish there was a good book about your favorite soccer player. If you wrote a book about him or her, then you would have written a biography. Because a biography is written about a real person and about that real person's real life, a biography is a nonfiction book. There are so many biographies that you may have noticed these nonfiction books are even given their own special section in the library.

Can you think of any biographies you have already read? Can you think of any biographies you would like to read that you haven't read already?

Directions: Match each person to his or her description on the right. Next, with the help of your librarian or teacher, go to the library and see if your library has a biography about any of these people.

If the answer is yes, color in the bubble with the person's name on this worksheet.

1. **George Washington**

a. She was an Indian who helped the early settlers at Jamestown.

2. **Christopher Columbus**

b. She is credited with helping make the American flag.

3. **Betsy Ross**

c. He was the famous explorer who discovered the Americas.

4. **Pocahontas**

d. He was the first president of the United States.

Autobiographies

An autobiography is a book written about someone's life. In an autobiography, the book is about the author who is writing the book. For example, if your favorite movie star wrote a book about his or her life, then it would be an autobiography. If you wrote a book about your life, it would also be an autobiography. Autobiographies are nonfiction books because they are not fiction; they are books that are not pretend. Because there are so many autobiographies, the library usually does not put these books with the other nonfiction books. Instead, these books are given a special section in most libraries. Autobiographies are interesting nonfiction books because you can learn so much about a person.

Part I

Directions: Read each statement. Write **True** or **False** on the line provided.

________ **1.** An autobiography is a fiction book filled with information that is not true.

________ **2.** An autobiography is a nonfiction book.

________ **3.** If you wrote a book about your life, it would be a biography.

________ **4.** Autobiographies are usually given a special section in most libraries.

________ **5.** If you went to the library, you would not be able to find any autobiographies.

Part II

Directions: Why do you think someone would want to write a book about his or her life? Use complete sentences for your answer.

____

____

____

____

Ride Like the Wind!

Directions: Read the following nonfiction story, then complete the activity below.

Cowboys

Have you ever watched a movie about cowboys? Movies make being a cowboy seem like it is nothing but fun. But in real life, being a cowboy was hard and dirty work. Cowboys had to round up cattle, brand the cattle, and ride over hot, dusty prairie land. Many of these cowboys didn't even own the horses they rode. Most cowboys did own their own saddles, but saddles were expensive. A saddle cost most men about a year's wages.

The word "chuck" is cowboy slang for food. The chuck wagon did indeed carry food, as well as water, cooking utensils, medicine, tools, and spare saddles. Cowboys usually got enough to eat, but it was the same food over and over: beef, bread, and beans.

Being a cowboy was definitely different than how it is shown on television.

Directions: Inside the lasso below, write five facts you have learned about cowboys.

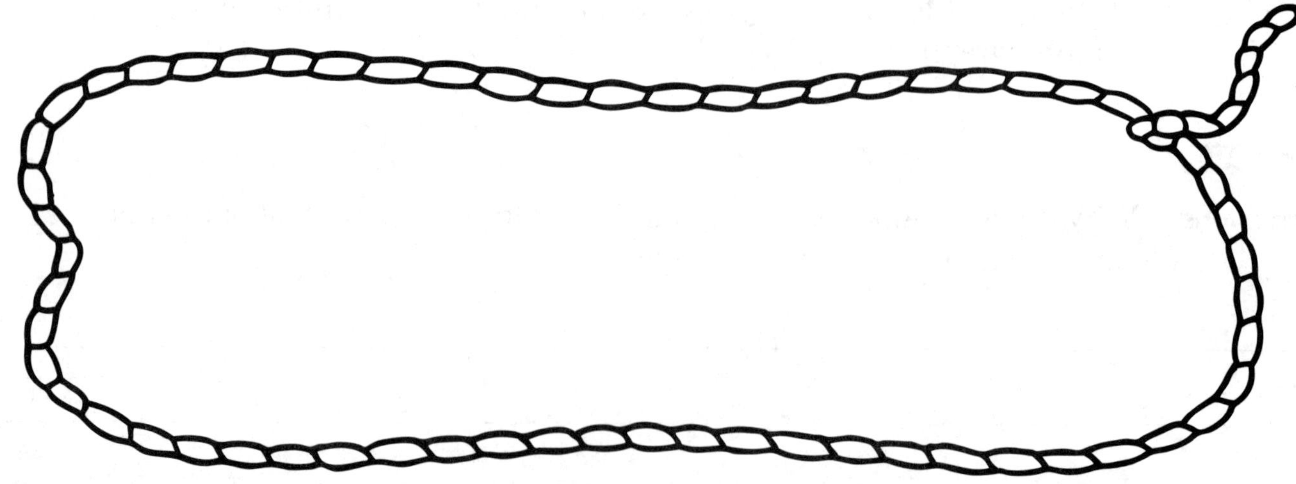

Just For Fun: On the back of the page, draw a picture of you as a cowboy or cowgirl.

A Dark and Spooky Place

Directions: Read the nonfiction story below, than answer the questions that follow.

Mammoth Cave

Mammoth Cave is a very interesting place to visit. Located in the state of Kentucky, Mammoth Cave is the largest cave in the world. It has about 330 known passageways, but there are at least a couple hundred more that have not been mapped. This cave even has an underground river where eyeless fish live. There are also blind shrimp, crayfish, crickets, and beetles in the cave. All of these creatures have highly developed senses to make up for their lack of vision.

1. Why would Mammoth Cave be an interesting place to visit?

____

____

2. Why do you think the animals in Mammoth Cave do not have eyes or are blind?

____

____

3. List two facts you learned about Mammoth Cave:

Fact #1: ___________________________________

____

Fact #2: ___________________________________

____

Working with Directions

Knowing how to write directions is an important skill. Directions are a type of nonfiction writing. There are directions for almost everything you do. Even something as simple as brushing your teeth has a set of directions.

Try your hand at seeing how well you can write directions for some everyday activities.

Directions: Choose one of these three activities and write directions on how to do this activity. Then follow the directions below.

| sharpening a pencil | tying a shoe | putting on a coat |

____

____

____

____

____

____

____

Directions: Using only the directions you have written, see if someone else in the class can follow your directions and do what you have asked.

Helpful Hint: The person may already know how to do what you have written about, but he or she cannot do anything except what you have written! He or she cannot add to the directions.

When you are finished, talk to your partner about changes you could make in your directions to help make the task easier to do.

Biography Autobiography | Fantasy Folktales | Nonfiction | Poetry | Fiction

How to Get There

There are many types of directions. Directions are a type of nonfiction writing. One kind of direction is the type that tells someone how to get somewhere. An atlas is often used to help someone decide how to make his or her journey. Another big help is the Internet, where someone can request a map with the quickest time or the shortest route to a favorite destination.

Directions: Write directions on how to get from your classroom to either the cafeteria or the library. When you are finished writing the directions, draw a picture of your final destination (where you ended your trip).

Making It Simple

Directions are a very important type of nonfiction writing. Most people like directions that are simple. When a person writes directions, he needs to get to the point but add enough detail so that someone can follow the instructions.

Directions: Pretend you need to write directions for a student who is new to your school. The directions should explain five things the students should do before lunch break.

Draw a picture to help explain each thing a little better.

Example: _Sharpen your pencil before the bell rings at 7:45._

1. ______________________________

2. ______________________________

3. ______________________________

4. ______________________________

5. ______________________________

Can You Follow Them?

Nonfiction writing gives information; therefore, directions are a type of nonfiction writing. Directions should be clear and easy to follow.

Directions: Follow the directions below. Put a check next to each direction after you complete it. The first one has been done for you.

☑ Draw a circle.

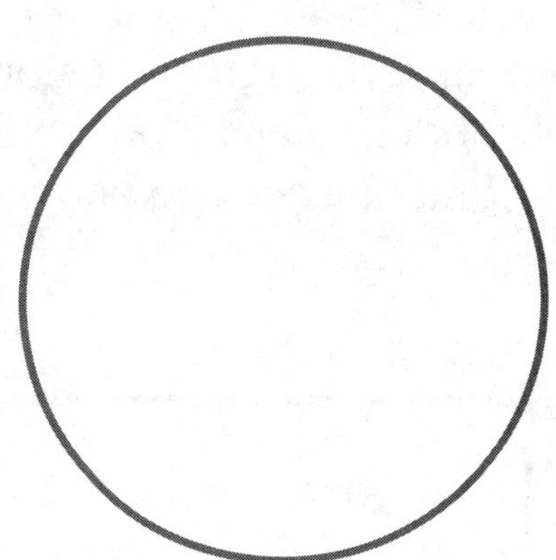

❑ Color the circle yellow.

❑ Draw a happy face inside the yellow circle.

❑ Underneath the circle, draw a square.

❑ Color the square blue.

❑ Use a green crayon and write your name inside the blue square.

❑ Write the name of your school underneath the blue square.

❑ At the top of this paper, write your name. Then draw a smiley face beside your name because you are finished with these directions!

School Writing

One important type of nonfiction writing is the writing found in schoolbooks or textbooks. Textbooks are often used in classrooms by teachers and students to help them study a subject and to learn information. For example, a math textbook would be filled with information about math. What type of information do you think a textbook used in a computer classroom might have?

Directions: Design and color a cover for the textbook below. Pretend the textbook is a science book. Once you are finished with your cover. List five topics or ideas that you might find in a science book. Don't forget the title for your book.

1. _______________

____

2. _______________

____

3. _______________

____

4. _______________

____

5. _______________

____

All in School

Nonfiction writing is important in any school. Nonfiction writing gives the reader more information about a subject. In school, students are often given books called textbooks. These schoolbooks are usually not found in the library, but instead they are books the students can keep with them or keep in the classroom for the entire school year. Each book covers a certain class subject and is filled with important nonfiction information.

Directions: You have just been given a very special assignment. A publisher has just asked you to help write something for one of its new science textbooks!

Choose one topic from the list below. With the help of your teacher or librarian, research the topic. Then in the space below, write 10 things you have learned about the topic. You can write the information you find as a paragraph or as a list.

| planets | energy | plants | animals | rocks | weather |

1. ____

2. ____

3. ____

4. ____

5. ____

6. ____

7. ____

8. ____

9. ____

10. ____

Something Extra: On the back of this page, draw a picture to go with your writing.

Subject Matters

In school, you study many subjects, and you often use textbooks to help you learn more information about these subjects. These textbooks are wonderful sources of nonfiction.

Directions: Read each short paragraph below. Choose from the books to help you decide which textbook the information might have come from. Write the name of the subject on the line provided.

__________ 1. Mercury is the closest planet to the sun, but it is not the hottest planet in our solar system. Venus, which is the second planet from the sun, is by far the hottest.

__________ 2. Triangles have three sides. Squares have four sides. In a square all the sides are equal in length. A rectangle also has four sides, but all sides are not equal in length.

__________ 3. It is important to eat the right portions from all the major food groups. It is also important to get plenty of exercise and rest each day.

__________ 4. You should always use correct capitalization when you are writing. Capitalizing is important because it helps make your message clear to the reader.

__________ 5. Be sure to take care of your supplies. Brushes should always be rinsed. Do not leave any paint on the bristles. Organize your supplies so you will know where to find them.

Write About It

Nonfiction writing is fun because you learn while you read! If you want to learn more about bears, you need to go to a nonfiction book that has information about bears. If you want to know how to fly a kite, you need to read a nonfiction book that has information about kites. In your classroom you have nonfiction books that give you information. These nonfiction books are called textbooks.

Part I

Directions: Write down the titles of any textbooks you use. Add more lines, if needed.

____

____

____

____

____

Part II

Directions: Imagine you had the chance to learn about anything you wanted to while you sit in class each day.

✎ *What topic do you wish you could have in a textbook?* _______________________

Now draw a picture of the topic you have chosen.

Writing References

Reference books are an important type of nonfiction writing. A reference book is there to help you learn more information about a certain topic. An atlas, an almanac, and an encyclopedia are all forms of reference nonfiction.

Directions: Choose from the topics below, then write a short reference page about the topic. Remember, a reference page should be nonfiction or true writing. It should provide general information about the topic.

- *taking care of a pet*
- *being a good student*
- *eating healthy foods*

- *taking great vacations*
- *getting along with friends*
- *playing outdoor games*

My Topic: ____

Some things you need to know about this topic are _______________________________

____

____

____

These things are important because _______________________________________

____

____

Something Extra: On the back of this page, draw a picture of you doing the activity you wrote about.

Word Wise

Reference books are one type of nonfiction writing. Reference books are books of fact about specific topics. If you have ever used a dictionary, an encyclopedia, or an almanac, then you have used a reference book.

Directions: Pretend you have been asked to write one page for a new dictionary that is coming out next year. This dictionary is special, though, because you get to create new words and write the definitions for these new words!

In the space below, create six new words. Write definitions for each of these words.

Example: *sniffdoodle — a picture drawn to look like a dog's nose*

1. _______________________

2. _______________________

3. _______________________

4. _______________________

5. _______________________

6. _______________________

Something Extra: Use one of your new words in a sentence. Write it on the back of this page.

Same Thing

Reference books are a very important type of nonfiction writing. A reference book gives facts about a certain topic or subject. Some reference books, like encyclopedias, are updated yearly to keep the information current (up-to-date).

Directions: Look at the encyclopedia topics listed below. Circle three topics you think might have to be updated each year. Once you have chosen three topics, explain why you think they might have to be updated each year.

Example: _Space travel — Space travel is constantly changing and improving so there would always be new information about this topic._

George Washington	Music	Technology
Florida	Children	Valentine's Day
Science	Education	Apples
Medicine	Sports	Dogs

Topic	Why It Needs To Be Updated
1.	
2.	
3.	

Small World

A reference book is a nonfiction book filled with facts about a certain topic. If you have ever seen a dictionary or an encyclopedia, then you have seen a reference book. One type of reference book that you may not be as familiar with is a *thesaurus*. A thesaurus is a lot like a dictionary. It is a book of words, and the words are organized alphabetically. A dictionary gives definitions of words, but a thesaurus gives synonyms and antonyms of words.

Synonyms are words that are the same or similar in meaning. For example, a synonym for *beautiful* is *pretty*. *Antonyms* are words that are opposite in meaning. An antonym for *pretty* would be *ugly*. You can look up a word in a thesaurus, and the book will list synonyms and antonyms for the word you want to know more about.

Directions: Read each word. Write a synonym and an antonym for each word. Use a thesaurus if you need help.

Word	Synonym	Antonym
1. mean		
2. sweet		
3. cute		
4. nice		
5. little		
6. good		
7. large		
8. kind		
9. quiet		
10. funny		

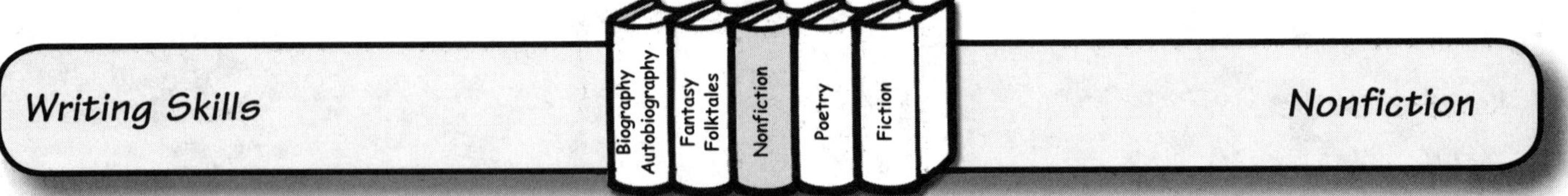

Dear Me

Do you like to get letters? Do you e-mail your friends and do your friends e-mail you? Does your grandmother send you a card whenever it is your birthday? If any of these things ever happen to you, then you already know how much fun it is to get mail.

Letter writing is one type of nonfiction writing. Usually in letters people share lots of facts and information about their lives. Could someone write fiction in a letter? Of course—but most of the time people write about real people, places, and events when writing a letter.

Directions: Use the space below to do some nonfiction writing of your own. Write a letter to your teacher telling what you like best about your class. Be sure to only mention things that really exist so that your writing is nonfiction and not fiction!

Writing History

One way you can learn about history is to read letters that were written in the past. Letters written in the past by real people who talk about real events are important pieces of nonfiction writing. Some authors use these letters to help them write books about certain time periods. Reading letters from the past is a lot like traveling in time!

Directions: Pretend it is 200 years into the future. Someone has discovered a letter you wrote 200 years ago! What would you want people to know about you or your time?

In the space below, write a letter to anyone you choose. Be sure to include details you would want someone in the future to know about you and your time.

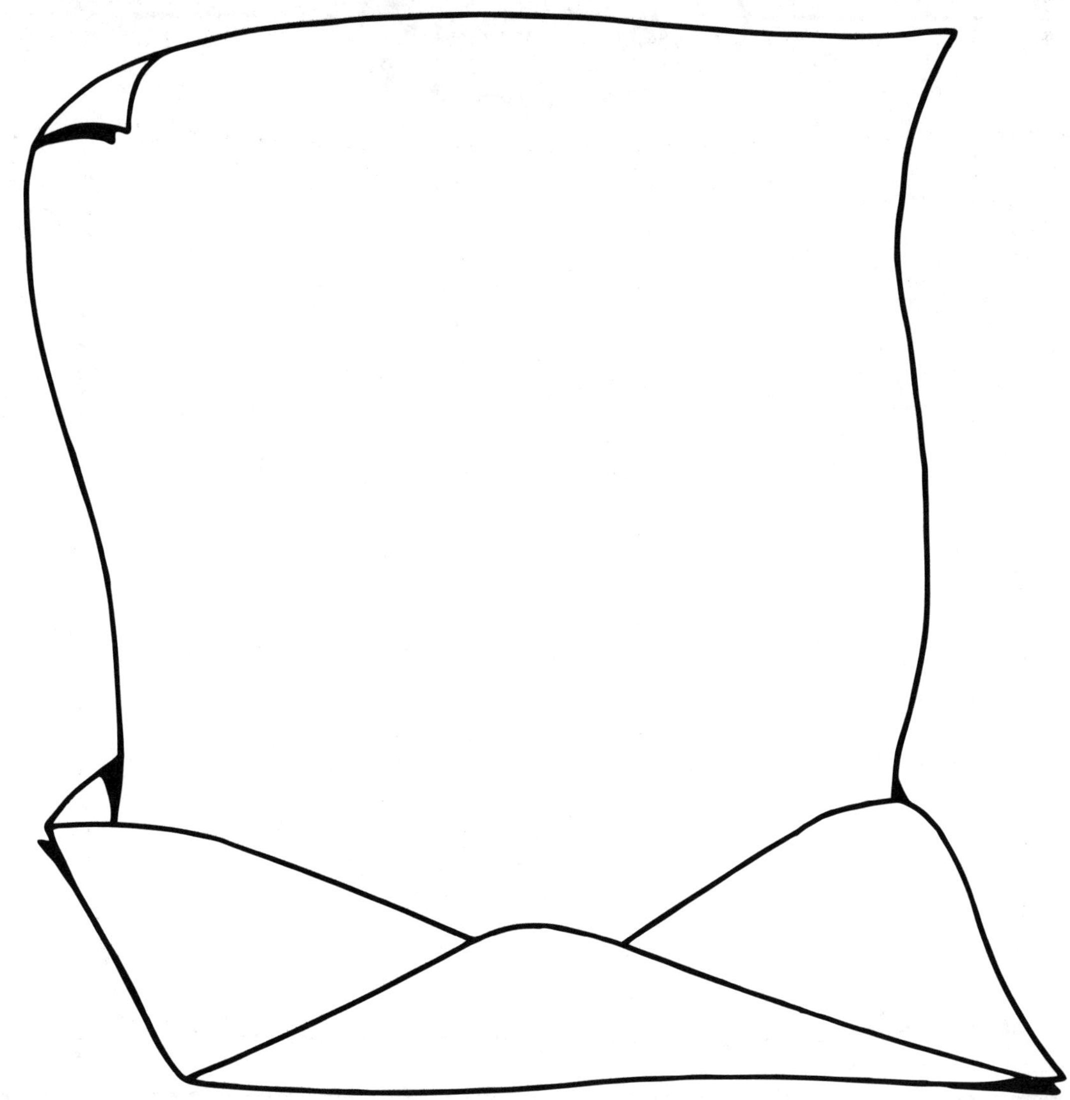

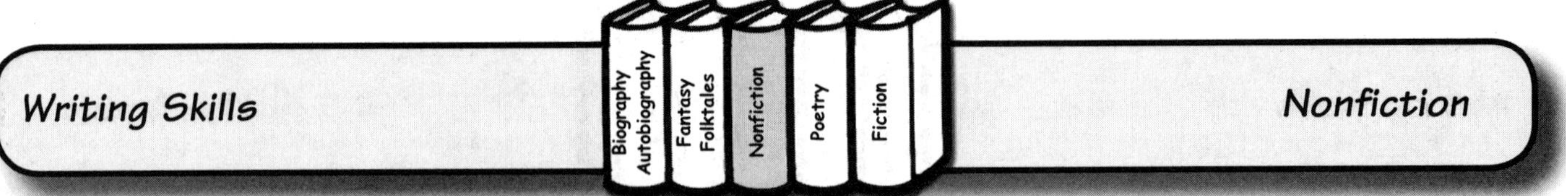

Document It

Cover Page

Many people write down what happens to them. Writing down the events that happen to you is called *journaling*. You can buy a fancy book to write in as a journal, or you can use plain notebook paper. The paper is not important; what is important is that you write!

Directions: Use the space below to design a cover for a journal. When you are finished, color the journal cover and cut it out along the dotted lines.

My Journal

Document It

Journal Page

Directions: Cut out the journal page below. Staple your piece of paper behind your journal cover. Once you have your new journal, write about what happened to you either yesterday or today.

Helpful Hint: If you like writing in your journal, you can add more paper for each day you want to write!

My Journal

Biography Autobiography • Fantasy Folktales • Nonfiction • Poetry • Fiction

The Five Ws

Newspapers are a major source of nonfiction writing. Newspaper articles are written to cover the five major *W*s. What are the five major *W*s? They are *who, what, when, where,* and *why.*

If you were a reporter and you wanted to write an article, you would have to write using the five *W*s, too.

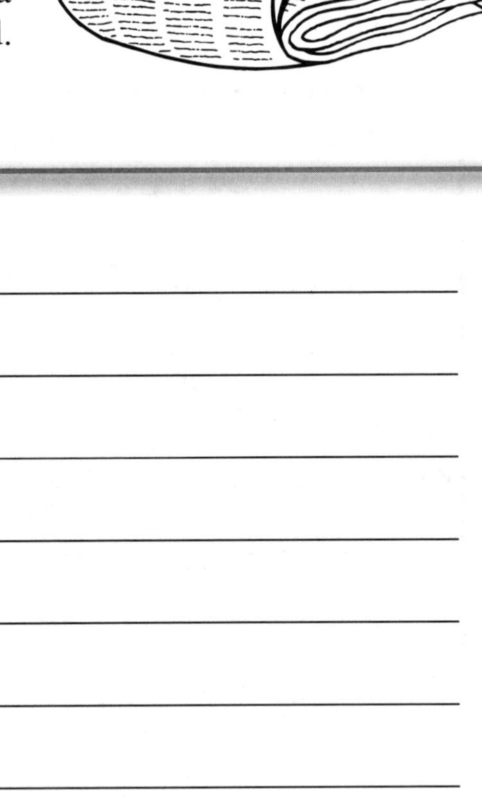

Directions: Think about something that has happened at your school. Maybe there was a pep rally or a dance or a class activity. Write an article explaining what happened. Be sure to answer each of the five *W*s.

The Event: ____

Who? ____

____

What? ____

____

When? ____

____

Where? ____

____

Why? ____

____

Headliners

One important type of nonfiction writing is the writing journalists do. Journalists often write for newspapers and magazines.

When a journalist writes an article, one important thing he or she must do is create a *headline*. A headline lets the reader know at a glance what the article will be about. A good headline will catch the reader's attention. It should be descriptive. For example, "Man Frantically Searches for Lost $1,000,000" is a better headline than "Man Loses Money."

Now see how you can do at writing some great headlines.

Directions: Decide what the article might be about by creating a headline. Fill in any blanks with words that will really get the reader's attention. You can put more than one word on each line.

SCHOOL TIMES

Woman Eats

____

SCHOOL TIMES

School Teacher

Discovers ______________

in the ________________

SCHOOL TIMES

______________ Digs

Up ____________________

SCHOOL TIMES

Students Invent

____

for

____

Something Extra: Choose one of the headlines you created. Then, on the back of this paper write a news story to go with it.

Caption Action

Have you ever heard the saying "A picture is worth a thousand words"? Pictures in nonfiction writing are very helpful in explaining what the written work is about and giving details at a glance. When pictures are used there are often words underneath the picture to quickly explain what is happening in the picture. These words are called *captions*.

Example: Firefighters try to rescue a young girl's cat. Fluffy was eventually rescued

and returned to her very happy owner.

Directions: Look at the following pictures. Write a caption for each one.

1.

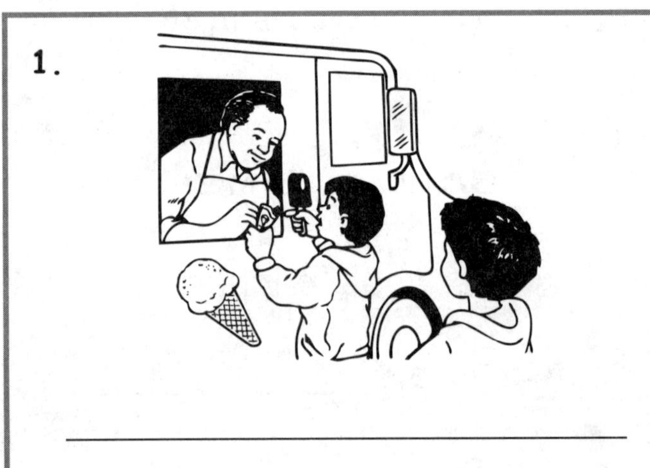

2.

3.

4.

72

Interview Me

Magazines are a popular form of nonfiction writing. Many of today's magazines contain interviews with famous people. If you could interview someone famous, who would you like to interview?

Directions: You may not be able to contact the famous person you would like to interview, but you are surrounded by interesting people each and every day who have plenty of things to say.

For the first part of this exercise, you will need to write a set of interview questions for the person you are about to interview. With your teacher's help, you will need to team up with a partner to complete this activity.

Once you know who your partner is going to be, think of five questions you would like to ask him or her. Prepare your questions below, but do not write the answers yet.

Once you have your five questions and your partner has his or her five questions, the two of you need to decide who will ask his or her questions first. As your partner answers your interview questions, write down his or her answers underneath each question.

I am interviewing ____

1. Question: ____

   Answer: ____

2. Question: ____

   Answer: ____

3. Question: ____

   Answer: ____

4. Question: ____

   Answer: ____

5. Question: ____

   Answer: ____

Joking Around

Magazines are a popular form of nonfiction writing. There are many different types of magazines written about many different subjects.

One popular page found in some magazines is a joke or comics page. This page will have funny things celebrities have said or funny pictures, riddles, rhymes, or jokes.

Directions: Create a fun page for a magazine. You can write jokes, draw funny pictures, or even write about something funny that has happened to you.

Helpful Hints: Never hurt someone's feelings trying to be "funny." Only tell jokes that would be fine to tell at school. If you are not sure about something, ask the teacher or simply do not include it on your magazine page.

Class Clown Magazine

____
(today's date)

Joke Corner

Picture Place

____
____
____
____

Funny, But True!

____
____
____

Everyday Things

You see nonfiction writing all around you every day. In the morning when you read the writing on your cereal box, you are seeing nonfiction writing. When you read the directions on your tube of toothpaste, you are reading nonfiction writing.

Try your hand at writing some directions on how to use some everyday things.

Directions: Look at the pictures below. Circle three of the picture choices. Then on the back of this paper, write directions on how to use each item you have circled.

Me, Myself, and I

You probably know yourself better than you know anyone else in the world. That is why it is easy to write about you!

Directions: Use the space below to write about you. Use the questions to help.

1. What is your name?

____

____

2. What are your favorite things to do?

____

____

3. Can you describe your family?

____

____

4. Who is your teacher, and what is the name of your school?

____

____

5. What are three things that are important to you?

____

____

6. What is one more thing you can tell that is all about you?

____

____

Hobby Time

Many people have hobbies. A *hobby* is something someone learns more about whenever he has extra time. Collecting coins is a hobby, and so is riding a skateboard.

Directions: Think about what you like to do in your spare time. What are your hobbies?

Write down some of your hobbies in the box to the right.

Now choose just one of your hobbies and write down six facts you know about it.

My hobby is ____

1. ___________________________________

4. ___________________________________

2. ___________________________________

5. ___________________________________

3. ___________________________________

6. ___________________________________

Something Extra: On the back of this page, draw and color a picture of your hobby.

Writing Facts

A good nonfiction writer knows how to write facts. A fact is something that can be proven.

Directions: Look at each opinion and change it into a fact.

Example: All chocolate is gross. (*opinion*)

Some people like chocolate and some people do not. (*fact*)

1. *Opinion:* Red is an ugly color.

Fact: ____

____

2. *Opinion:* Girls love chocolate ice cream.

Fact: ____

____

3. *Opinion:* She is the nicest teacher in the world.

Fact: ____

____

4. *Opinion:* Summer is the best season.

Fact: ____

____

5. *Opinion:* Dogs are the best pets.

Fact: ____

____

6. *Opinion:* Books are better than movies.

Fact: ____

____

Examine It Closely

A fact is something that can be proven. An opinion may or may not be true. Although it is okay to write about your opinion, many nonfiction writers deal mostly in facts. If a writer of nonfiction were going to write a book about wolves, he would need to be sure to present the facts to his readers and not just his own opinion about these animals.

Directions: Read each set of sentences. Fill in the circle next to the one that is a fact and not an opinion.

1.
   (a) There are many different types of insects.

   (b) All insects are creepy.

2.
   (a) Spiders are mean creatures.

   (b) Spiders spin webs and use them to catch food.

3.
   (a) All insects can only live or survive in the outdoors.

   (b) Some insects have wings.

4.
   (a) Some famous cartoon characters are drawn as insects.

   (b) Cartoon insects are too scary for little children.

5.
   (a) Spiders have eight legs.

   (b) Insects have eight legs.

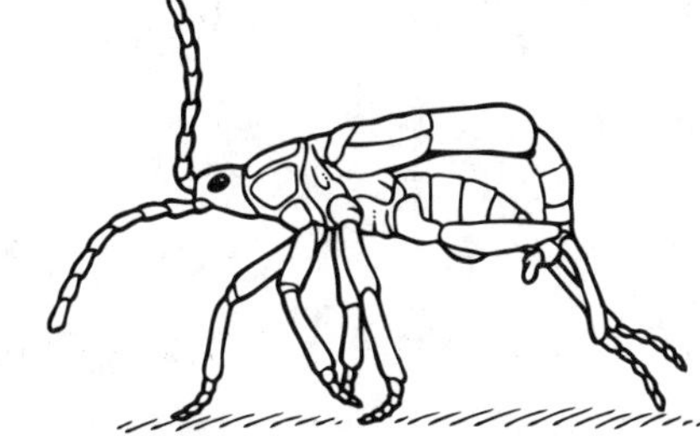

Something Extra: On the back of this sheet, write five fact-and-opinion sets of your own. Then ask another student to guess which one is a fact and which one is an opinion.

You, You, You

Nonfiction writing is filled with facts or things that are true. One topic you can write lots of facts about is you. Nobody knows you better than you. If someone asked you when your birthday is and you told the person the date of your birthday, that's a fact. A fact is something that is true. You can practice writing nonfiction by learning how to write some facts about you.

Directions: Listed below are six numbers. Inside each number, write one fact about you. When you are finished writing, color each number.

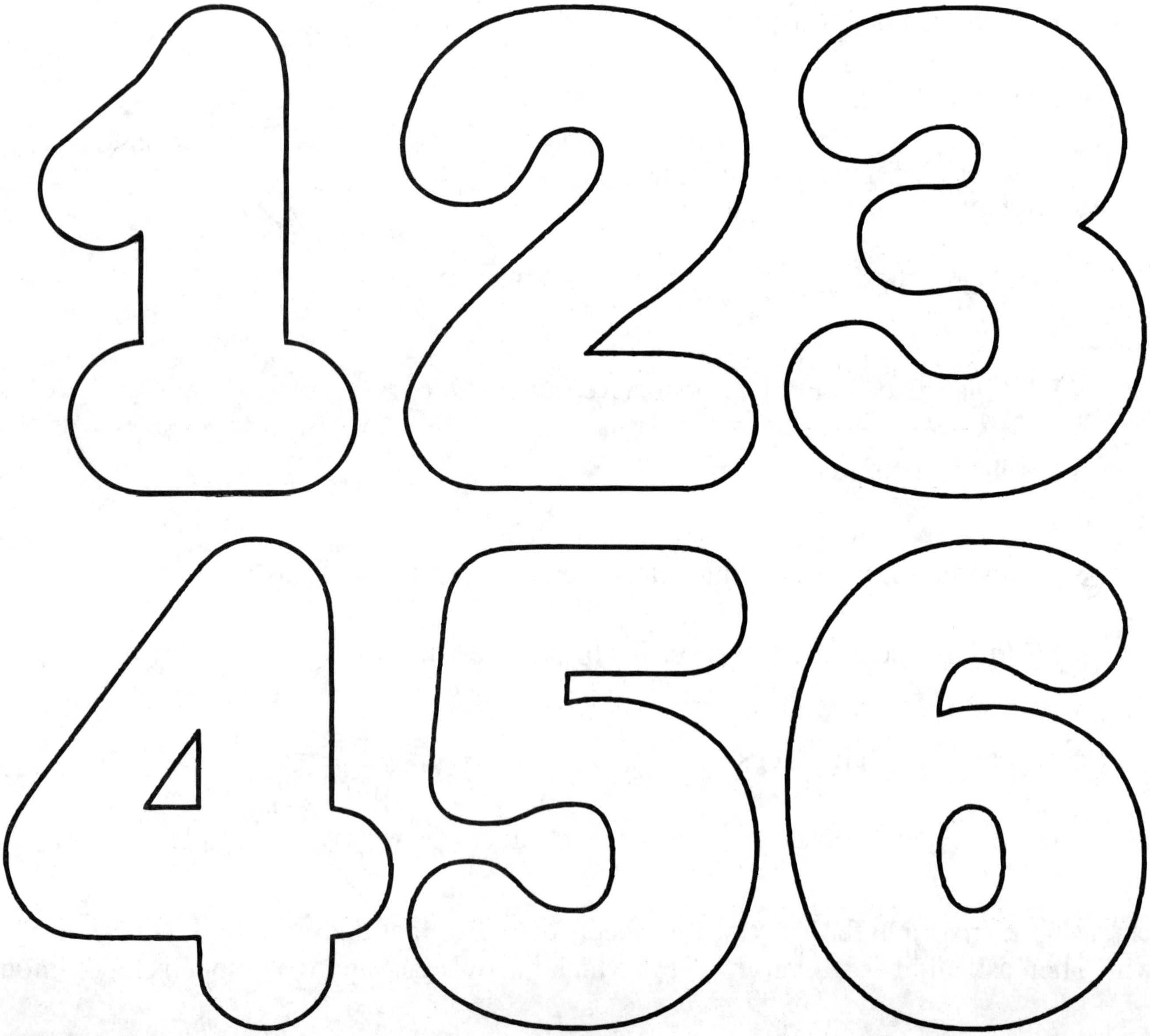

Starting Off Right

A good writer knows a good start is a must when writing nonfiction. All good writers know to start each and every sentence with a capital letter. Use your good writing skills to help these sentences start off right.

Directions: Read each sentence. If the sentence is capitalized correctly, write the letter **C** on the line provided. If the sentence is incorrect, rewrite the sentence as it should be written.

__________ **1.** bears are some of the best-known animals in the world.

____

____

__________ **2.** Bear cubs stay with their mothers for up to four years.

____

____

__________ **3.** a bear's sense of smell is better than a human's.

____

____

__________ **4.** polar bears are excellent swimmers.

____

____

__________ **5.** American black bears climb trees to find food.

____

____

Something Fun: On the back of this page, draw and color a picture of you with a teddy bear or a real bear!

Ruff! Ruff!

Sometimes it is rough being a writer. You have to make sure that what you are writing is not only interesting but also written correctly. See if you can figure out how to make good writing a little less rough by helping out some friendly dogs. (Ruff! Ruff!)

Directions: Look at the dogs below. These dogs will not stop barking! They are trained to bark whenever they see writing mistakes. See if you can quiet down the dogs by correcting the mistakes.

Read each set of sentences that are given. Circle the dog that has the sentence that is correctly written.

1.

 Some people think dogs make great pets.

 some people think dogs' make great pets.

2.

 do you have a pet dog?

 Do you have a pet dog?

3.

 dogs can come in many shapes, sizes, and colors.

 Dogs can come in many shapes, sizes, and colors.

4.

 Some dogs do special jobs or services for people.

 some dogs do special jobs or services for people.

5.

 Many dogs shed their heavy winter coats to get ready for the warmer months.

 many dogs shed their heavy winter coats to get ready for the warmer months.

Knowing How to End It

Good nonfiction writers know that the ending of something is just as important as the beginning. It is certainly important to know what type of ending punctuation to use whenever you are writing.

There are three types of ending punctuation:

✎ Use a period (.) when ending a statement or a mild command.
   Example: My feet are cold.

✎ Use a question mark (**?**) when asking a question.
   Example: Why are my feet so cold?

✎ Use an exclamation point (**!**) when showing excitement.
   Example: There's a snake crawling on my feet!

Directions: Read each nonfiction sentence. Rewrite each sentence and add correct ending punctuation.

1. There are seven days in every week

____

____

2. Monday starts the school week

____

____

3. Do you think Friday is the best day of the week

____

____

4. How wonderful it is when your birthday is on the weekend

____

____

5. Wednesday is in the middle of the week

____

____

End Points

Nonfiction writing is interesting to read, but it would be hard to read if there were no ending punctuation marks.

A good writer knows how to use a period (**.**), a question mark (**?**), and an exclamation point (**!**) correctly.

Directions: Read the following true story about the famous poem "Paul Revere's Ride." There are 10 ending punctuation mistakes. Circle each mistake and add the correct punctuation.

"One If by Land, and Two If by Sea"

"Paul Revere's Ride" is a famous poem written by Henry Wadsworth Longfellow This poem tells the story of Paul Revere, a hero of the American Revolutionary War

Paul Revere was a silversmith who, on the night before the battle of Lexington and Concord, rode across the Massachusetts countryside warning that the British troops were moving toward them

"One if by land, and two if by sea" are the words Longfellow used to describe the signal Paul Revere would use Revere watched a church tower to find the signal One light in the church tower meant the troops were coming by land What do you think two lights meant

Because Revere made his famous ride, everyone was warned that night The next day they were ready to fight the British How brave Paul Revere must have been to make his famous ride

---

From Start to Finish

Nonfiction writing is writing about things that are true. Read the true statements below and see if you can help make them grammatically correct from start to finish.

Directions: On your mark, get set, and go! Look at each sentence below. There is one mistake in each sentence.

✎ Find the mistake.

✎ Circle the section of the sentence that has the mistake.

✎ Correct the mistake.

Example: (m)y running shoes are covered in mud.

1. Being a good runner takes lots of practice

2. a marathon is a long race in which many people run at the same time.

3. The boston Marathon is a well-known race.

4. Runners must drink lots of water?

5. running is a good type of exercise.

6. A runner must wear a good pair of running shoes?

7. if you plan to run in a marathon, you must train for the event.

8. How wonderful it would be to win a marthon.

Icky E-mail

Letter writing is a popular form of nonfiction writing. Many years ago, it took months for letters to reach their destination. Today, because of the Internet, letters can be e-mailed and reach their destinations instantly. Just be careful when you send your own e-mails that you are still using your good grammar skills!

Directions: Read the following e-mail.

✎ Highlight any capitalization mistakes with a *green* crayon.

✎ Highlight any ending punctuation mistakes with a *red* crayon.

✎ Highlight any spelling mistakes with a *yellow* crayon.

Can you guess what happened to me while I was babysitting

I wuz watching this cute little girl named Kara. She wanted to play a gamme. While i was in the living room setting up a game for us to play, Kara snuck into the kitchen. she opened a bottle of syrup and poured it all over the entire kitchen!

it took me three hours to get the icky mess off of everything Luckily, by the time Kara's mom came home, everything was clean, but things did still smell a little sweete.

Kara's mom paid me my money, but it was the hardest munney I ever earned.

Alphabetically Correct

Encyclopedias are an example of reference nonfiction. Encyclopedias categorize information alphabetically. New encyclopedia sets are published each year to keep the information in the books up-to-date.

Directions: Look at the encyclopedia entries below. They are all out of alphabetical order. Write the entries in their correct alphabetical order.

Out of Alphabetical Order	In Alphabetical Order
1. Tennessee	1.
2. Congress	2.
3. Pilgrims	3.
4. butterflies	4.
5. insects	5.
6. sports	6.
7. basketball	7.
8. movies	8.
9. cats	9.
10. space	10.

Going to the End

A good nonfiction writer knows he must finish whatever he starts. No one wants to start reading a book only to find out it has no ending! See what you can do to help finish some sentences.

Directions: Ricky Writealot has writer's block. He was writing an article for the local newspaper about your school, but something has happened to him, and now he can't think of how to complete his sentences! If he doesn't get his notes finished soon, he will not be able to write his article and then he will not meet his deadline with the newspaper.

See if you can help finish Ricky's writing so he can look over his notes and go write his article for the paper.

Helpful Hint: Don't forget to add ending punctuation to Ricky's notes.

✎ The name of the school is ____ .

✎ The teacher of this class is ____ .

✎ ____ is the school's mascot.

✎ ____ is the name of their principal.

✎ ______________________ is something they serve in the cafeteria . . . a lot.

✎ ______________________ , ______________________ , and ______________________
are three people who go to this school.

✎ The librarian's name is ____ .

✎ School is finished at ______________________ o'clock.

See It More Clearly

A good writer uses lots of descriptive words. Adjectives are words that are used to describe nouns. An adjective tells how many, which one, or what kind of noun or pronoun. For example, a writer could write this sentence: *There is a girl.*

This is an okay sentence, but it doesn't give any information. There are no adjectives to describe the girl. Now look at this sentence.

✎ *There is a tall, beautiful girl with long, curly hair.*

This is a better sentence because it gives information about the girl. The adjectives *beautiful* and *tall* help the reader form a better picture of the girl, and the adjectives *long* and *curly* also help describe her hair.

Directions: Look at each noun. List two adjectives that could be used to describe it.

Example: dog

1. car

2. homework

3. summer

4. movies

5. vegetables

6. games

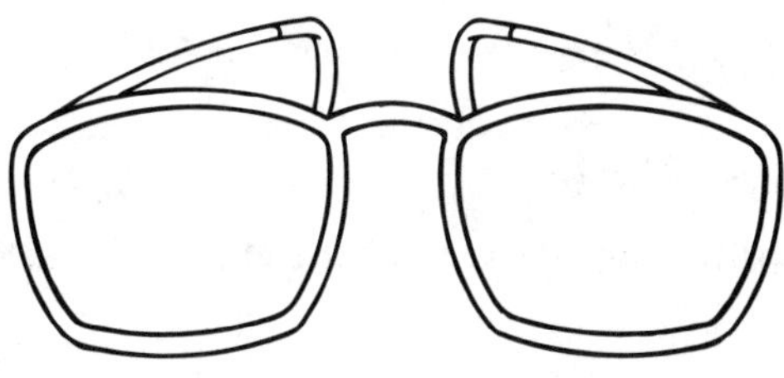

Helping to Describe

An adjective is a word that helps describe or give more information about a noun or a pronoun. Good writers use adjectives to help their writing be more descriptive.

Directions: Read the following encyclopedia entry. Finish the entry by adding adjectives where they are needed.

Dogs

A dog can come in _______________________ sizes. Some dogs are large, and

some dogs are _______________________ . Dogs need owners who like them and

are willing to play with them. Dogs definitely need _______________________

owners.

Some dogs do not have owners. These stray dogs can often be

_______________________ and _______________________ . You should

never approach a dog you do not know. Always stay away from any

_______________________ looking dogs. Being the owner of a dog can be a lot

of fun. But a dog owner must be a _______________________ and

_______________________ person.

Something Extra: On the back of this page, write five sentences of your own about a pet. Be sure to use at least one adjective in each sentence.

Gross! Finding the Subject

When an author writes a nonfiction book, she has a certain subject in mind. Maybe she is writing about a certain time in history. Maybe she is writing an entry for an encyclopedia. Or maybe she is writing about a certain type of animal.

When an author writes a sentence, she also has a subject in mind. Every sentence has a subject, just as every nonfiction book has a subject. The subject of a sentence is who or what the sentence is all about.

Example: The boy ate a slimy worm.

Who is this sentence about? It is about the boy. Therefore, *boy* is the subject of the sentence. What did the boy do? He ate a slimy worm. Delicious!

Directions: Read over each of these gross sentences and find the subject. Choose a crayon by picking a color you think is really gross. Use this crayon to circle the subject in each sentence.

1. Chloe blew her nose on the sleeve of her shirt.

2. Kayla Beth ate sardines for breakfast.

3. Gage played in the mud.

4. Brett cleaned dirt out from between his toes.

5. Sandra made candles using earwax.

6. Kaycee burped the entire alphabet.

7. Emilee caught flies on her tongue.

8. Daniel ate caterpillars for lunch.

Just For Fun: On the back of this paper, draw and color a picture of you catching flies on your tongue.

Verbs in Action

Good writing has lots of good action words. These action words are called verbs. These are the words that help add action to a story. Words like *kick, jump, hop, smile, laugh,* and *scream* are all examples of action verbs.

Part I

Directions: Think about action verbs that you use in your life. List as many as you can on the lines below:

____________________   ____________________   ____________________   ____________________

____________________   ____________________   ____________________   ____________________

____________________   ____________________   ____________________   ____________________

Part II

Directions: Choose five of the action verbs you listed and write a sentence using each one.

1. ____

2. ____

3. ____

4. ____

5. ____

Part III

Directions: Draw a picture of you doing one of the action verbs you listed.

Hooking Up Subjects and Verbs

All sentences have a subject and a verb. The subject is who or what the sentence is all about. The verb usually shows the action in the sentence, and it sometimes links the subject to something on the other side of the sentence.

Examples: Mom baked cookies. (*Mom* is the subject. *Baked* is the verb.)

Mom is a great cook. (*Mom* is the subject. The word *is* links mom to being a great cook, so *is* acts as the verb.)

Directions: Look at each fishing boat. Decide which fish needs to be caught to complete the sentence. Color the fish that is the correct choice. Write the correct word on the line.

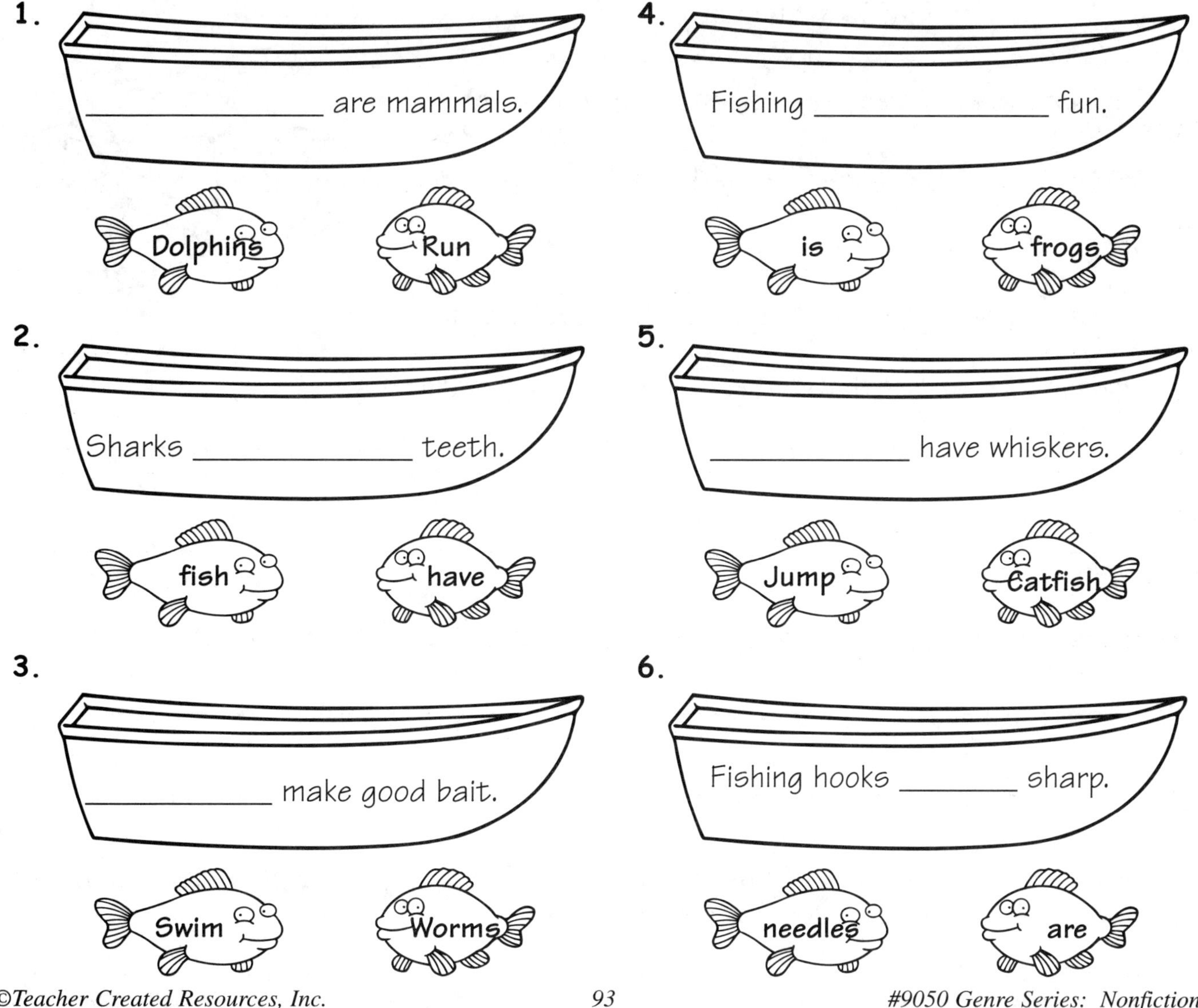

Spell It ~~Rite~~ *Right*

All good writers know it is important to spell words correctly. Good spelling makes a story easier to read and easier to understand. Whether a writer is writing fiction or nonfiction, she still must carefully proofread her writing for spelling mistakes.

Directions: Read over the following information from a nonfiction book about turtles. Correct any spelling mistakes you find by writing an **X** on each misspelled word. Then rewrite the words correctly on the lines below. You can use a dictionary if you need to.

Tortoises and Turtles

by Sally Morgan

Tortoises and turtles are ancient anumuls that furst appeared on Earth more than 200 million years ago, when the dinosaurs wur alive. Their appearance haz changed very litttel in all this time. They are eazy to recognize becuz they have a heavy shell covering their backk.

---

1. _______________________

2. _______________________

3. _______________________

4. _______________________

5. _______________________

6. _______________________

7. _______________________

8. _______________________

Just For Fun: On the back of this sheet, draw and color a picture of what Earth might have looked like more than 200 million years ago.

Spell-Check

When you write something on a computer, the computer will often use "spell-check" to check your spelling for you. If you have spelled a word wrong, it will signal you that something is wrong, and you may want to look at the word again. However, spell-check cannot always catch everything. Spell-check will not catch a mistake if a person has spelled the word correctly but simply used the wrong word.

For example, if you wrote, "Eye went to the store" but you meant to write, "I went to the store," spell-check will not recognize the word "eye" as incorrect. That is why even with computers, you still need to be a good speller!

Directions: Look at the following sentences. Spell-check could not find the mistakes. See if you can. Circle the mistakes, and then write each sentence correctly on the lines provided.

1. Hour friends are very nice.

____

____

2. There friends are nice, too.

____

____

3. There was a sail on juice at the grocery store.

____

____

4. Do you want to go, oar do you want to stay?

____

____

5. For her birthday she got too puppies.

____

____

The Diary Cow

Directions: Look at the diary cow. Write a diary entry on the side of the cow about a day you might have spent in the country. Only include events that could really happen on a farm. (In other words, do not have aliens come and visit you!) Be sure to use correct spelling and punctuation.

When you are finished, color and cut out your picture of your diary cow.

The "Bear" Facts About Commas

Good nonfiction writers know how to use commas correctly. One important way to use commas is with items in a series. If a writer lists three or more things, she needs to have commas to separate the items. The job of each comma is to separate the items so the list is not confusing to the reader.

Examples: I like ice cream, spaghetti, and pizza.

I want to visit Florida, Georgia, Maine, Texas, and Alaska.

Helpful Hint: Notice there is always one less comma than there are items in the series.

Directions: Read each sentence. Add commas wherever they are needed.

1. American black bears can actually be black brown or white!

2. There are many types of bears, including polar bears panda bears and black bears.

3. Bears' strong teeth can grab crush and chew their food.

4. Polar bears can be found in Alaska Canada Russia Denmark and Norway.

5. Many bears can climb run and swim.

6. Bears will protect their cubs from wolves mountain lions and humans.

7. A female bear can have one two or three cubs at a time.

8. Polar bears like ice snow and cold weather.

Commas and More Commas

All good writers use commas to help make their writing easier to understand. One way to use commas is to separate items in a series. A comma is used to separate items if there are three or more items in a series.

Example: My favorite restaurants are Jake's Place, Gage's Diner, and Sally's Sub Shop. The commas let you know there are three separate restaurants being discussed.

Directions: Complete each list below. Use commas as needed.

1. List three colors: ____

2. List three days of the week: _______________________________________

3. List three months of the year: _____________________________________

4. List three planets: ____

5. List three animals: ____

6. List three fruits: ____

7. List three vegetables: ____

8. List three sports: ____

9. List three school subjects: ____

10. List three holidays: ____

1 , 2 , 3 · 1 , 2 , 3 · 1 , 2 , 3

Finding Commas in Nonfiction

Newspapers and magazines are filled with nonfiction articles. A good writer knows he has to use commas when writing to help make his writing easy to understand. Newspaper and magazine columnists also must know how to use commas correctly. One important way to use commas is to separate items in a series. If three or more items are listed, the writer must use commas to separate them.

Example: I like to read sports' articles about soccer, baseball, and basketball.

Notice that the commas in the example above are used to separate the different sports.

Now that you know how to use commas, get your teacher to help you complete the activity below. You will need the materials listed to complete this activity.

Materials:

- old newspapers and magazines
- scissors
- glue

Directions: Look through a magazine or old newspaper. Find at least 10 examples where the writer used commas with items in a series. Cut out the examples and glue them in the spaces below.

1.	2.
3.	4.
5.	6.
7.	8.
9.	10.

Looking for Everything

Directions: Circle any spelling, capitalization, ending punctuation, or comma mistakes you find. Rewrite the sentences correctly on a separate sheet of paper and staple that paper to this sheet.

1. 

2. 

3. 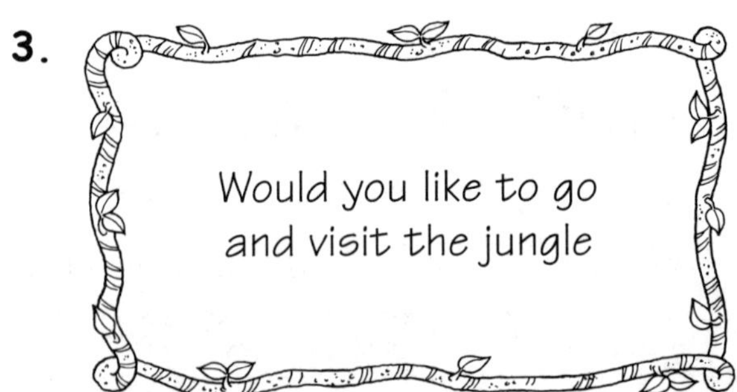

4. 

5. 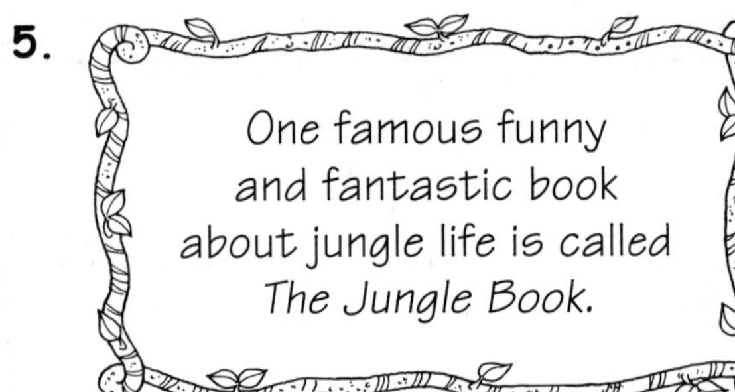

6. 

7. 

8. 

Test Your Knowledge

Teacher Directions

Materials:

- "Teacher Directions" (below and page 102)
- "Questions and Answers" (page 103)
- pencils
- scissors
- two boxes
- five chairs
- timer
- small prizes
- list of students' names, cut into individual strips and placed in one box
- timer

Directions: This is a game called "Test Your Knowledge." You can use this game with any subject, but it works especially well once you have finished the unit of study on the nonfiction genre.

✎ Make a classroom set of copies of "Questions and Answers" (page 103). Give each student a copy. Tell each student to write down four questions and their correct answers. Students are to write their questions in the spaces provided on the handout. The questions must be about something each student has learned during his/her unit of study. The questions must be facts. The students must also include the answers.

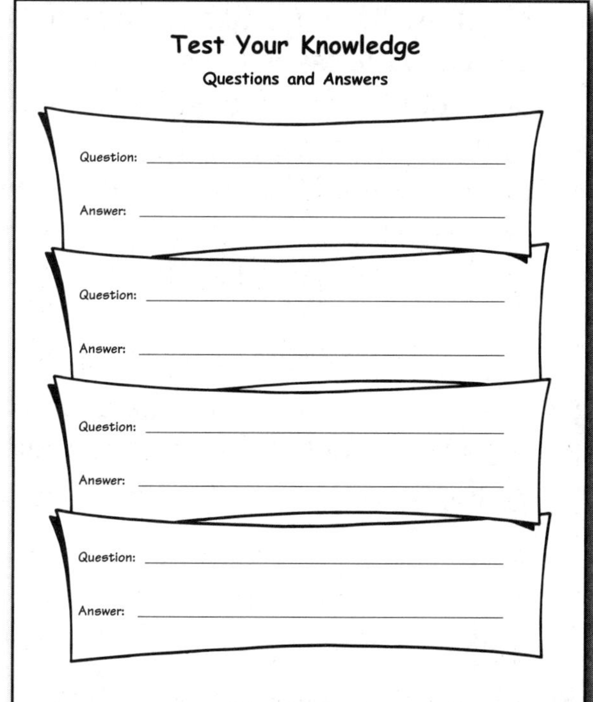

Test Your Knowledge

Teacher Directions *(cont.)*

✎ When the student has completed all four questions and answers and cut them out, he or she should show them to the teacher so the teacher can quickly verify that the questions are good and the answers are accurate. Once this is done, place the questions and answers in the box labeled "Test Your Knowledge."

✎ When everyone has finished the "Questions and Answers" worksheet, draw five students' names from the name box. Have these five students sit in five chairs in front of the class. Decide on an amount of time for the game (25 minutes is a good suggested time). Tell the students that when the timer goes off, the students sitting in the five chairs by the end of the game will be the winners.

✎ Next, draw one more name from the name box. Have this student look at the five students and decide which student he would like to challenge. Have him name the student. Have him draw a question from the question box without looking at the question and hand it to the teacher. The teacher will read the question out loud. If the student who has been challenged can answer the question correctly, he keeps his seat. If the student cannot answer the question, the student who challenged him now has a chance to answer the same question. If he answers the question correctly, he takes the seat and the other player returns to a regular seat in the classroom. If neither student answers correctly, both students go to a regular seat in the classroom, and the teacher draws a new name to fill the empty seat. The teacher should then tell what the correct answer was to the old question since a new question will now be drawn. Reminder: Student names go back in the box to be drawn again and again. Questions and answers already asked, however, do not go back in the box.

✎ The game continues in this manner until the timer goes off. Once the timer goes off, the students left in the five seats win the game. It is up to the teacher to decide an appropriate prize for the winning players.

Test Your Knowledge

Questions and Answers

Question: ____

Answer: ____

Question: ____

Answer: ____

Question: ____

Answer: ____

Question: ____

Answer: ____

Color Me Purple

Directions: Read the information beside each balloon. If the information is true about nonfiction, then color the balloon *purple*. If the information is not true, write an **X** on the balloon.

1.

◯ Encyclopedias are a type of nonfiction.

◯ Encyclopedias are a type of fiction.

2.

◯ Nonfiction can be described as writing that is made-up or make-believe.

◯ Nonfiction can be described as writing that is true or not make-believe.

3.

◯ The opposite of nonfiction is fiction.

◯ The opposite of nonfiction is autobiography.

4.

◯ A nonfiction writer gives information to his reader.

◯ A nonfiction writer does not give his reader any information.

5.

◯ Historical documents are not an example of nonfiction.

◯ Historical documents are an example of nonfiction.

6.

◯ A letter written by the Wicked Witch of the East would be an example of nonfiction writing.

◯ A letter written by the Wicked Witch of the East would not be an example of nonfiction writing.

Something Extra: Draw a big balloon on the back of this page. Write a fact inside the balloon that you know about nonfiction writing. (Make sure the fact is not one already listed on this page.) When you are finished, color the balloon any color you like.

Nonfiction Knowledge

Directions: Read each question. Fill in the circle next to the correct answer.

1. The word *nonfiction* means ________________.

   a "writing that is real"   **b** "writing that is not real"

2. The prefix "non" means ______________.

   a "not"   **b** "super"

3. There are many different types of nonfiction writing.

   a true   **b** false

4. One type of nonfiction writing is ________________.

   a folktales   **b** reference books

5. Encyclopedias are examples of ________________.

   a fiction writing   **b** nonfiction writing

6. Letters and diaries can be nonfiction writing if ________________.

   a they are written by and about pretend people

   b they are written by and about real people

7. Newspaper articles are examples of nonfiction writing that are all about __________.

   a past events   **b** current events

8. The directions on a tube of toothpaste are an example of ________________.

   a fiction writing   **b** nonfiction writing

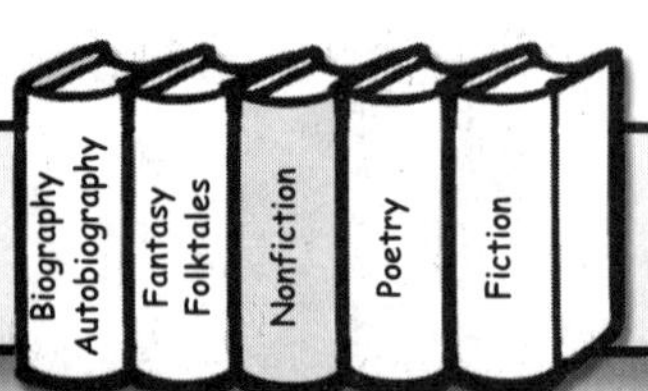

Fact Cards

Directions: Complete each fact card.

Fact Card #1

List three types of nonfiction writing that you have studied.

Fact Card #2

Tell what the prefix "non" means.

Fact Card #3

What type of nonfiction books gives definitions of words?

Fact Card #4

If you wanted to learn more about life in China, would you look in the fiction or nonfiction section of the library?

Fact Card #5

Give an example of a book you use at school that would have nonfiction writing.

Fact Card #6

An atlas is a nonfiction book. What is an atlas?

Something Extra: On the back of this page, draw your own fact card. Write down three nonfiction facts you know about your school.

A "Real" Test

Directions: Read and answer each number.

1. Define *nonfiction.* _______________________________________

____

2. What is the difference between fiction and nonfiction?

____

____

3. Give at least three examples of types of nonfiction writing.

____

____

4. Give an example of one type of writing that would *not* be nonfiction.

____

5. List a type of nonfiction book that would be found in a library's reference section.

____

Something Extra: Writing directions is a type of nonfiction writing. In the space below, write directions on how to do something that you do every day!

What I do: ____

How I do it: ____

____

____

The Facts

Part I

Directions: Nonfiction writing is filled with facts or things that are true. Read each statement below. If it is a fact, write the **Fact** on the line. If it is not a fact, write **Not a Fact** on the line.

__________________ **1.** There are seven days in a week.

__________________ **2.** There are 12 months in a year.

__________________ **3.** February is the best month of the year.

__________________ **4.** School work is so easy!

__________________ **5.** School work is so hard!

__________________ **6.** The word "school" has six letters.

__________________ **7.** You should eat both fruits and vegetables.

__________________ **8.** The best fruit of all is strawberries.

__________________ **9.** Wednesday is the worst day of the week.

__________________ **10.** A dog is the best pet to have.

Part II

Directions: Read each statement. Rewrite each statement so it becomes a fact.

Example: Monday is the best day of the week.

Monday is the first day of the week.

1. Steak is the best meat. ____

2. Blonde hair is the prettiest hair color. _______________________________

3. Ice cream is the best dessert. _____________________________________

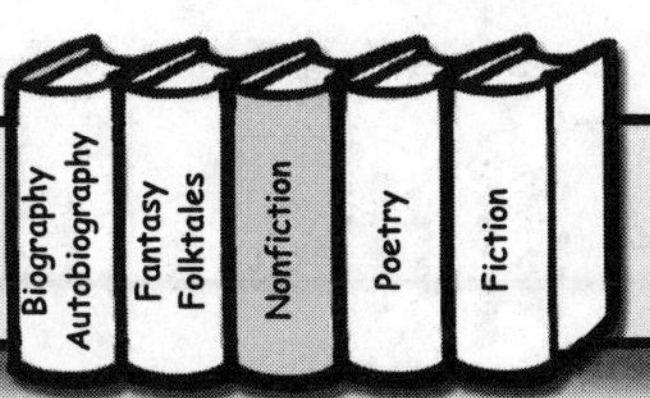

Circle It In

Nonfiction is writing that is about real people, places, things, and events. Fiction writing is just the opposite. Fiction writing is about things that are pretend or make-believe. A nonfiction writer has to deal with facts. Facts are things that can be proven to be true. There are many different types of nonfiction writing. Directions, reference materials, and newspapers are all examples of nonfiction writing.

Directions: Read each statement and darken in the circle of the correct answer.

1. Nonfiction writing is writing about __________________.

   (a) things that are make-believe   **(b)** things that are real

2. Nonfiction writing is about real people, places, things, and __________________.

   (a) events   **(b)** dreams

3. A nonfiction writer deals with __________________.

   (a) facts   **(b)** fantasy

4. One example of nonfiction writing is __________________.

   (a) newspaper writing   **(b)** comic-book writing

5. If you were reading directions, you would be reading __________________.

   (a) nonfiction   **(b)** fiction

6. Writing that is the opposite of nonfiction is __________________.

   (a) fiction   **(b)** journal writing

7. Reference materials are an example of __________________.

   (a) fiction writing   **(b)** nonfiction writing

8. A fact is something that can be proven to be __________________.

   (a) false   **(b)** true

It Could Happen

Events Page

Nonfiction writing is filled with events that are true or that could or have happened. Nonfiction writing is not pretend or make-believe. Writing that has make-believe, or events that are not real, is called fiction.

Directions: Look at the events listed below. Use the "Real or Not?" worksheet (page 111) and then decide under which column each event should be placed on that page. Cut out the events below and glue them to the chart. Be sure to glue the events in the correct column.

An alien will come today and take you back to his planet.	It will rain this year.
A teacher will teach your class.	A talking dog will teach your class.
The sun will shine this year.	The moon will decide to take a vacation at the beach.
You will have a birthday this year.	Goldilocks and the three bears will invite you over for some porridge.
A fairy godmother will come and offer you three wishes.	You will eat a meal this week.

It Could Happen

Real or Not?

Real Event (Nonfiction)	Not a Real Event (Fiction)

Something Extra: Draw and color a picture of one of the events from either column.

Information in a Donut

Directions: Look at the donuts below. Color only the donuts that have information that is true about nonfiction writing.

1.

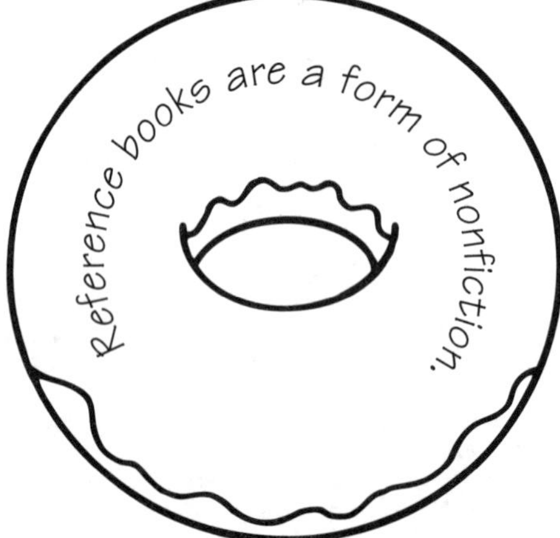

2.

3.

4.

5.

6.

Read and Answer

Directions: Read the following nonfiction story. Then answer the questions that follow.

The Highest Mountain in the World

The highest mountain in the world is Mt. Everest. Mt. Everest is 29,028 feet (8,848 m) high. On May 29, 1954, Edmund Hillary and Tenzing Norgay were the first men to reach the top. The first woman to reach the top was Junko Tabei on May 16, 1975.

Mt. Everest reaches up so high through Earth's atmosphere that the air at the top is very thin. There is not enough oxygen to maintain life. Most climbers need bottled oxygen to help them breathe.

1. How high is Mt. Everest? ____

2. Why do most people need oxygen when they climb Mt. Everest? ______________

   ____

3. Who were the first men to reach the top of Mt. Everest?

   ____

4. In what year did the first woman reach the top of Mt. Everest? ______________

5. Why do you think someone would want to climb Mt. Everest?

   ____

   ____

6. Have you wanted to do something that someone thought you couldn't do? ________

   If you answered "yes," what was it? ______________________________________

   ____

Picturing Nonfiction and Fiction

Writing that is nonfiction is writing that is based on truth or facts. Fiction is writing that is based on make-believe. One way to understand nonfiction is to realize that it is anything that is real. You are a real person living a real life and not a make-believe one. So, if you wrote about your life, it would be a nonfiction story.

Some people understand things better when they see them. To help you understand nonfiction and fiction better, try drawing some nonfiction and some fiction scenes.

Directions: Look around you. What do you see? Use half of the space below to draw exactly what you see from where you are sitting. Draw as many details as you can. Then, on the other side of the page, draw the same picture but add some imaginary items to the picture. For example, maybe there is a fairy floating over your head or an alien hiding in someone's backpack.

Nonfiction	Fiction

Mix and Match

Part I

Directions: Draw a line to match each word to its definition.

1. nonfiction

2. non

3. fact

4. directions

5. true

a. nonfiction writing that tells how to do something

b. something that is true

c. not false

d. prefix that means "not"

e. writing that is based on facts

Part II

Directions: Use the space below to write five facts about the months of the year and/or the days of the week.

1. ____

2. ____

3. ____

4. ____

5. ____

Read and Answer

Directions: Read the following nonfiction story and answer the questions that follow.

Sequoyah

Sequoyah was a Cherokee Native American. He was born in Tennessee. The Cherokees did not have a written alphabet to write anything down about their tribe. Everything that was learned had to be told to someone else and memorized. Can you imagine never being able to write anything down? Can you imagine a world with no books? Well, this is how the Cherokees lived until Sequoyah decided there was a problem that needed solving.

Sequoyah created a written language for the Cherokees. He made an alphabet in which 85 symbols were used for Cherokee sounds. The written language Sequoyah invented is still being used today.

1. Who was Sequoyah? ________________________________

2. Where was he born? ________________________________

3. What problem did Sequoyah think needed to be solved? ________________

____

4. How many symbols does Sequoyah's alphabet have? ________________

5. Do you think having an alphabet is important? Explain your answer.

____

Cookies! Cookies!

Directions: Read this short story and then follow the directions below.

A Delicious Mistake

Have you ever eaten a chocolate chip cookie? Over 7 billion chocolate chip cookies are eaten every year. Did a great cook set out to create the chocolate chip cookie recipe? No—it was all a mistake!

In 1930, Ruth Wakefield was busy running her Toll House Inn. She mixed up a batch of cookies and discovered that she was out of her baker's chocolate. She broke up some chunks of chocolate into small pieces, hoping that the chocolate bits would melt and go into the dough when she baked it. But when the cookies came out of the oven, she did not have her chocolate cookies; instead, she had chocolate chip cookies. What a delicious mistake!

Directions: Look at each statement. If the information is a fact, color the cookie that is next to it. If the information is not a fact, write an **X** on top of the cookie.

 **1.** Over 7 billion chocolate chip cookies are eaten each year.

 **2.** Chocolate chip cookies are everyone's favorite cookie.

 **3.** Ruth Wakefield invented the chocolate chip cookie.

 **4.** All of Ruth's customers at the inn hated her new cookies.

 **5.** Chocolate chip cookies were created in 1930.

 **6.** Ruth Wakefield was trying to make a pie when she created her chocolate chip cookies.

 **7.** Oatmeal cookies are better than chocolate chip cookies.

 **8.** Ruth Wakefield ran the Toll House Inn.

Act It Out

Directions: Have you ever played charades? In charades, you act out something to a crowd of people, and the people try to guess what you are doing. In charades, you cannot use any spoken words. This activity is like charades—but the good news is that you can speak!

With your teacher's help, divide into groups of two to three people. Then you and your group must decide on one of the topics below or chose a topic of your own. Do not tell anyone which topic you and your group have chosen.

The teacher will give you 15 minutes to organize your group. You and your group will choose a topic and then decide how to act it out so the class can guess which topic you are performing. You will then have the chance to watch other groups and guess what they are performing. Try to keep your skits fairly short.

Helpful Hint: Each of the topics has something to do with nonfiction, or things that are true.

Topic Choices

1. You are using a map to find your way on a vacation trip.

2. You are following directions on a box to cook a new recipe.

3. You are playing a musical instrument in a band.

4. You are playing on the playground at recess.

5. You are eating lunch in the cafeteria.

6. You are playing in a ballgame.

7. You are learning how to work a new math problem.

8. You are going to the library to check out a book.

9. You are going shopping at the mall.

10. You are watching television with your friends or family.

Fill in the Blanks

Directions: Use the Word Bank to help you fill in the blanks. Be sure to capitalize each word as needed.

Word Bank

alphabetically	true	newspaper
encyclopedias	directions	nonfiction
diary	fiction	

Nonfiction is writing that is about things that are real or (**1**) ________________ .
Fiction is just the opposite. (**2**) ________________ writing is about things that are pretend or not true.

There are many type of nonfiction writing. If you read the (**3**) ________________ on a tube of toothpaste, you have just read nonfiction writing. If you look at articles and information in a daily (**4**) ________________ , that is also nonfiction writing.
(**5**) ________________ writing can also be written in story form, but in this case, the story you read would be true.

Another popular type of nonfiction writing is writing in a (**6**) ________________ .
Many people write in a diary to keep up with what happens to them each day. If you have never tried to keep a diary, you should!

(**7**) ________________ are another type of nonfiction writing. In an encyclopedia, you can look up information about a variety of people, places, and things. Encyclopedias are organized from A–Z. This means they are arranged (**8**) ________________ .

Picture the Fact

Nonfiction writing is writing that is filled with information and facts.

Directions: Look at each picture. Then write two facts about what you see.

Example: 

1. <u>Dogs are mammals.</u>

2. <u>Dogs have four legs.</u>

1. __________

2. __________

1. __________

2. __________

1. __________

2. __________

1. __________

2. __________

1. __________

2. __________

1. __________

2. __________

Having a Ball

To "have a ball" is to have fun; and it's fun to read about people, places, and things!

Directions: Below are a lot of different balls. Each ball has space for you to write on it.

Now, think about how much you read every single day. Each time you read something that is nonfiction, write down a description of what you read. Try to write in as many balls as you can. Use the examples below to help you.

Helpful Hint: Since space is limited, you do not have to write in complete sentences.

Examples:

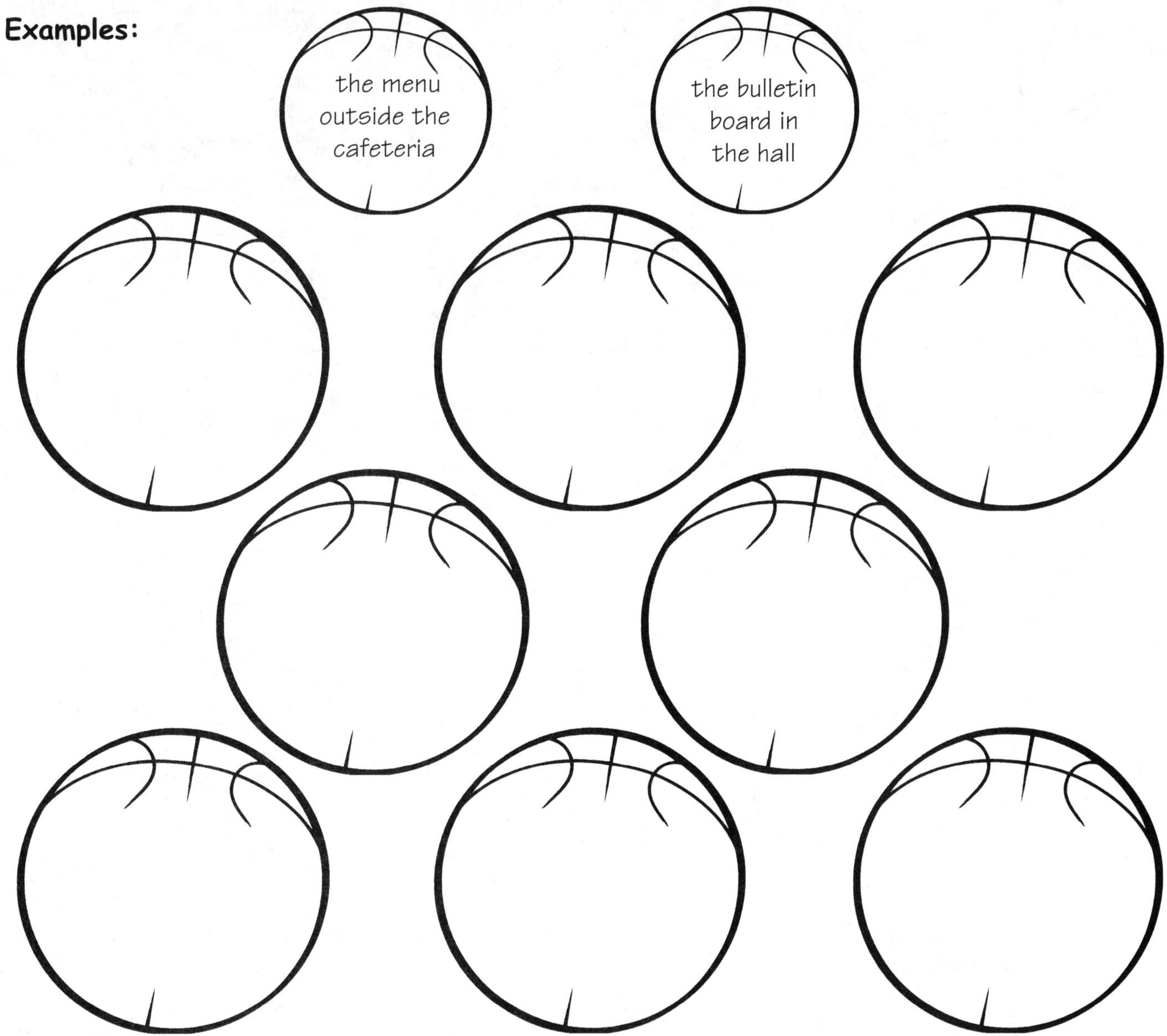

All Over the Globe

Directions: Only color the globes that contain something true about nonfiction.

1. Nonfiction writing is filled with facts.

2. A nonfiction story has many fantasy creatures.

3. An encyclopedia is a type of nonfiction writing.

4. Encyclopedias are organized alphabetically.

5. Dictionaries are a type of nonfiction writing.

6. A talking chicken might write a nonfiction story.

7. The opposite of nonfiction is fiction.

8. A fact is something that is not true.

9. A dragon and a fairy are nonfiction characters.

Finding Directions

Directions are a type of nonfiction writing. Directions are all around you.

Directions: Find three things that have directions written on them. Read the directions.
Then see if you can rewrite the directions in your own words.

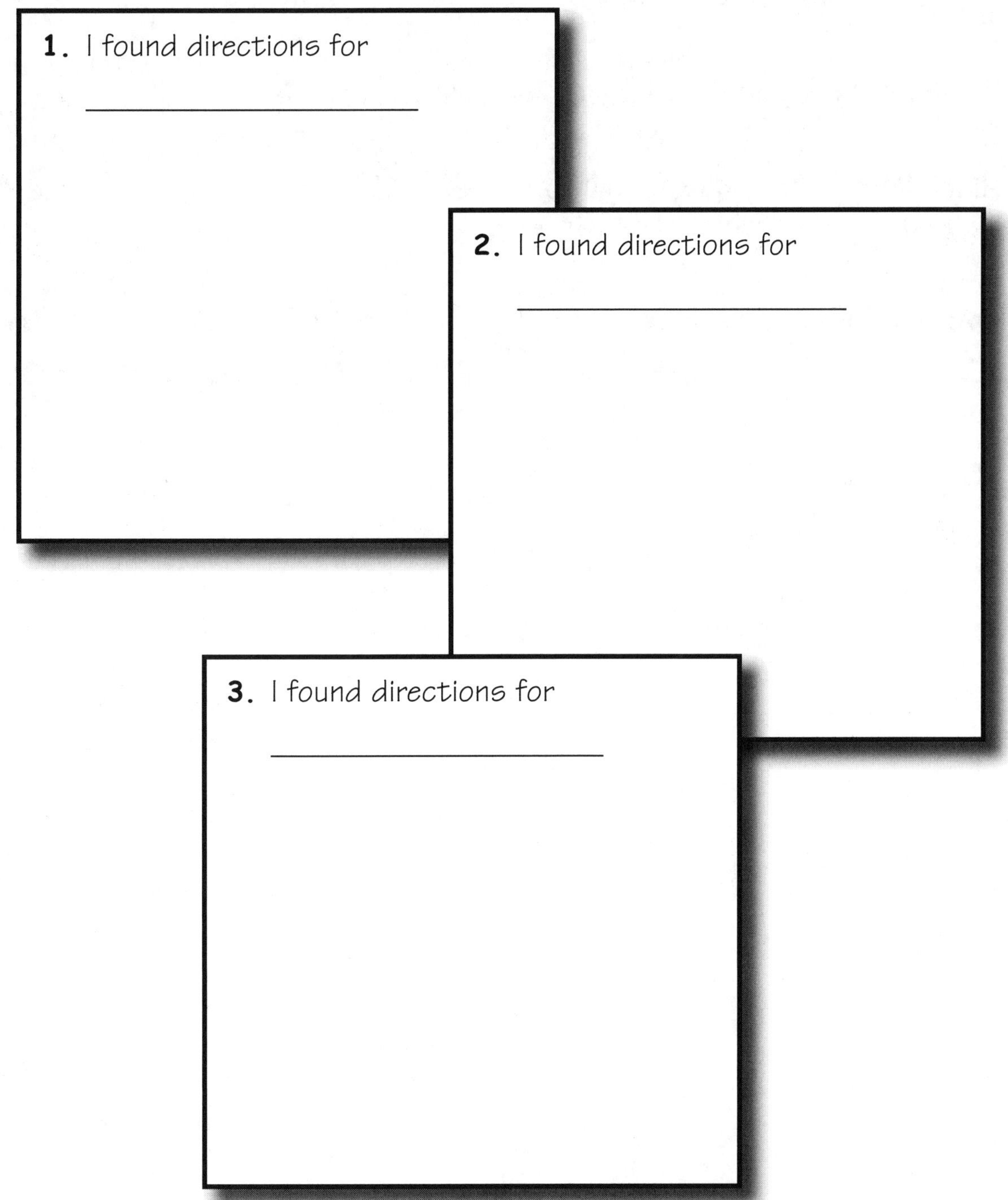

Easy Directions

Directions are a type of nonfiction writing, but writing directions is harder than it may seem. Try your hand at writing directions for some common things.

Directions: In the first space below, write directions for tying a shoelace. In the second space below, write directions for writing the letter "A."

When you are finished, get with a partner that your teacher has assigned you and see if your partner can follow your directions.

Helpful Hint: Your partner must follow *your* directions—even if he or she already knows how to do what is being asked!

How to Tie a Shoelace	How to Write the Letter "A"

Mapping the Directions

Being able to read, write, and even understand directions are all very important skills.

Prove you can do these things by following the directions below.

Directions: Draw a map showing how to get from your classroom to the area where you leave school at the end of the day.

In the first space below, draw the map. Below your map, write the directions.

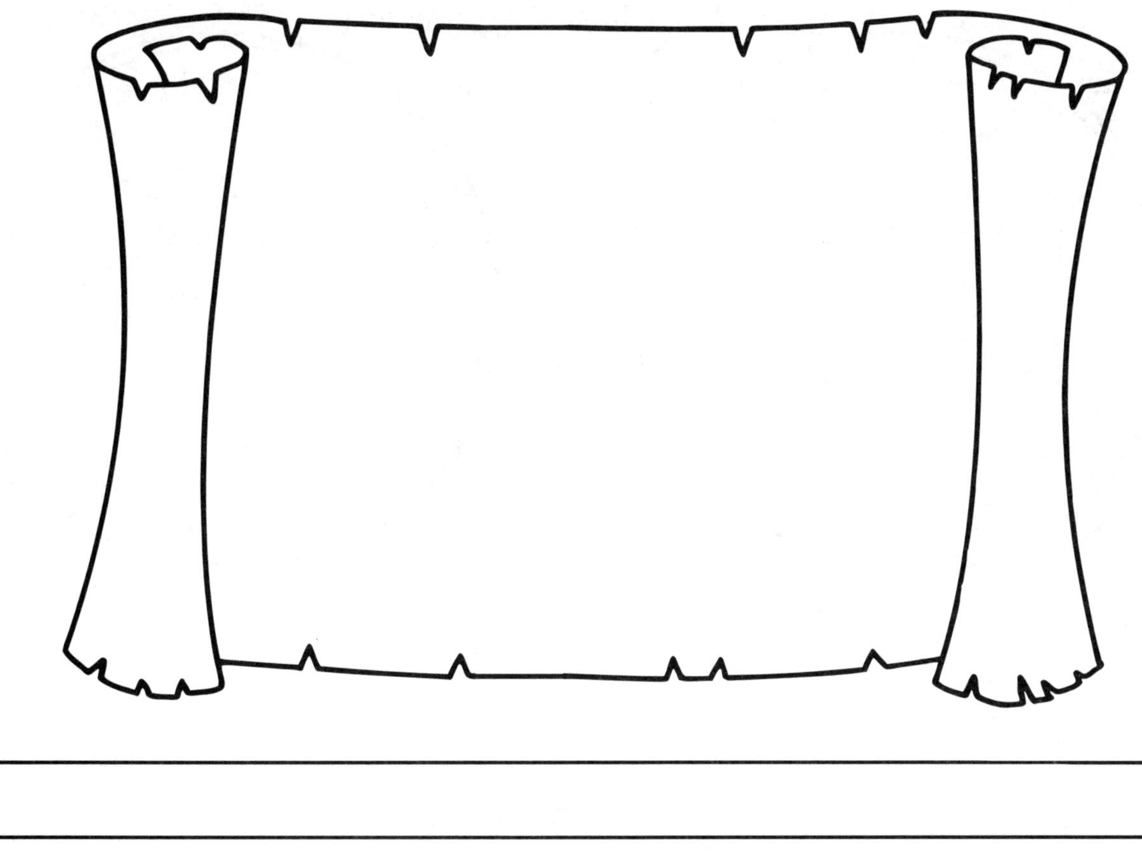

Fact-Finding Mission

Your schoolbooks contain lots of nonfiction writing. See if you can prove this to be true.

Directions: Choose two of your schoolbooks that you think have nonfiction writing. Look in these books for facts that prove they are nonfiction. Write the title of each book in a magnifying glass. Add your five facts on the lines provided.

Book Title

Book Title

Fact #1: _______________________________

Fact #2: _______________________________

Fact #3: _______________________________

Fact #4: _______________________________

Fact #5: _______________________________

Fact #1: _______________________________

Fact #2: _______________________________

Fact #3: _______________________________

Fact #4: _______________________________

Fact #5: _______________________________

Advertise for the Library

In many libraries, the nonfiction section of the library is often passed over. This is too bad because the nonfiction section is filled with fascinating, fact-filled books. But for some reason students still tend to go straight for the fiction books.

Use your talents to see what you can do to get your fellow students to pay more attention to the nonfiction section.

Directions: In the space below, design a poster advertising the nonfiction section of your library. Remember to have a catchy phrase and colorful, neat pictures.

What a Tail!

Directions: Below are pictures of animals with their tails missing! Go to the library and use an encyclopedia or another appropriate nonfiction source to look up each animal. Find a picture of the animal to see what the tail should look like. Then draw the tail of the animal on the picture. Be sure to color your animal, too.

As you look up each picture, write down two facts about each one that you learn while looking up each animal.

Giraffe

Fact #1: _______________________

Fact #2: _______________________

Elephant

Fact #1 _______________________

Fact #2 _______________________

Lion

Fact #1: _______________________

Fact #2: _______________________

Zebra

Fact #1 _______________________

Fact #2 _______________________

Paper-Plate Places

Encyclopedias are filled with information about places. Use an encyclopedia to help you complete the activity below.

Materials:

- paper plates
- crayons, markers, and/or colored pencils

Directions: What is your first name? What letter does your first name start with? Use the first letter of your first name to help you with this project. Get an encyclopedia that starts with the first letter of your first name. If someone else has the same encyclopedia, try using the first letter of your last name or else you may simply have to share!

- Look through the encyclopedia and find a place that is mentioned. It can be any city, state, country, etc.

- Use the paper plate your teacher has given you. Fold the paper plate into two equal parts with the line going horizontally (side-to-side) across the center of the plate.

- On the top half of the plate, write the name of the place you have found in your encyclopedia. Underneath the name, draw a picture of your place. Be sure to color your picture.

- On the bottom half of your plate, write a paragraph about your place. Write information you have learned from the encyclopedia.

- Write your name on the back of your plate, when you are finished.

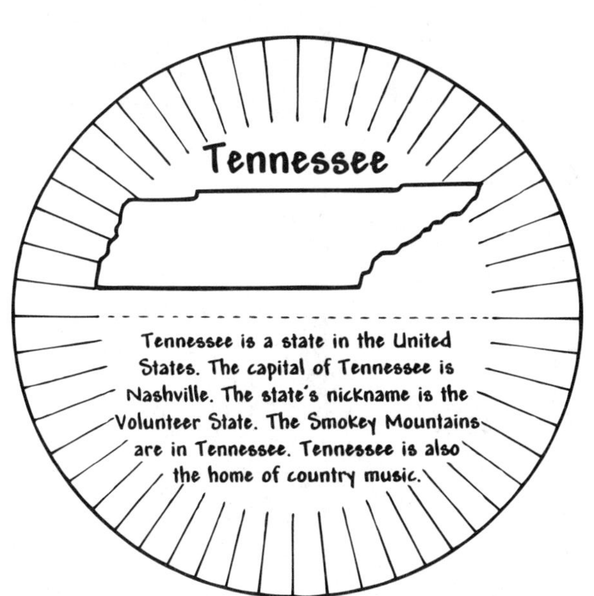

Dictionary Dash

Compete against your classmates to see who is the best at using a dictionary.

Materials: dictionary, pencil, paper

Directions: When your teacher gives the signal to begin, use your dictionary to find the words listed below as quickly as you can.

What do you do when you find the word? Do not write the definition. Instead, write the guide words. What are guide words? Guide words are the words at the top of the dictionary page that guide you alphabetically to find a word.

When you are completely finished, raise your hand so your teacher will know you are done.

Word	Guide Words	
1. cow	______________	______________
2. stop	______________	______________
3. summer	______________	______________
4. baby	______________	______________
5. go	______________	______________
6. cap	______________	______________
7. popcorn	______________	______________
8. pool	______________	______________
9. bear	______________	______________
10. tree	______________	______________

New Words

Dictionaries are a very important type of nonfiction writing. One important function of a dictionary is to give definitions of words. Each year, new words are added to the dictionary as they become part of our language.

Directions: Have you ever wanted to create some words of your own? Do you already use words that no else uses? For example, what if the word *turn* and *dump* were combined, and you created "tump"? How would you use the new word in a sentence?

✎ *He tumped over the glass of milk.*

Now it's your turn. Make new words by combining words that already exist. Come up with five new words this way, and then write the definitions of these new words.

Word	Definition
1.	
2.	
3.	
4.	
5.	

Something Extra: Now chose any one of your new words and use the word in a sentence.

____

____

Jotting in Your Journal

Instructions

Many people write nonfiction every day and do not even realize they are writing it. How? They write in a journal or diary. Writing each day in a journal is writing about real events that have happened. Since it is filled with facts or true events, it is nonfiction writing.

Directions: Use the paper your teacher gives you and keep a journal.

Helpful Hint: Do not write down anything that you would not want to share with someone else!

Be sure to write in your journal each day. You must write in your journal for five days. When you are finished, turn in your completed journal to your teacher.

Use the page given to you by your teacher to create a cover for your journal. Make the cover a reflection of you. In other words, design the cover with things you like. If you are a sports fan, put lots of sports pictures. If you love music, draw lots of music-related pictures on your journal cover. When you have your cover completed, staple the cover to the five sheets of journaling paper.

Jotting in Your Journal

Cover Page

Name: _______________________

MY JOURNAL

Jotting in Your Journal

Entry Page

Date: ____

My Journal Entry: _____________________________________

____

____

____

____

____

____

____

____

____

A Journal from the Past

Journal writing is some of the most interesting nonfiction writing that there is. People that keep journals have a written memory of things that happened in the past. Sometimes you think you will always remember something, but unless you write it down, the memory may not stay with you.

Directions: Your parents or grandparents may not have kept a journal when they were younger, but you can still help them capture some memories from the past. Conduct an interview with someone who is older than you by using the interview questions written below.

Write down his or her memories, and then after your teacher has seen your work, be sure to give the person your assignment as a keepsake.

Interview Questions for ________________________________

1. What is your earliest memory? ________________________________

____

2. What is one of your happiest memories? ________________________________

____

3. What is the best gift you have ever given or received? ________________________________

____

4. Do you have any special memories you would like to share about anyone in your family? If so, what are they? ________________________________

____

Something Extra: On the back of this sheet, draw and color a picture of the person you interviewed.

Letter for the Future

Many people like to read letters written by someone from the past. These letters give the reader a sense of what life was like long ago.

What if you could leave a letter for the future in a time capsule? What would you write? What would you say? Think about these questions as you do the following activity.

Materials:

- one sheet of light brown paper

- pencil

Directions: Write a letter to someone in the future. Tell them anything you would want them to know about what life is like now. Some things you might want to include in your letter might be the following:

✎ *your name and age*

✎ *where you live*

✎ *where you go to school*

✎ *information about your family*

✎ *any pets you have*

✎ *the cost of things today*

✎ *the technology that exists today*

✎ *what an average school day is like*

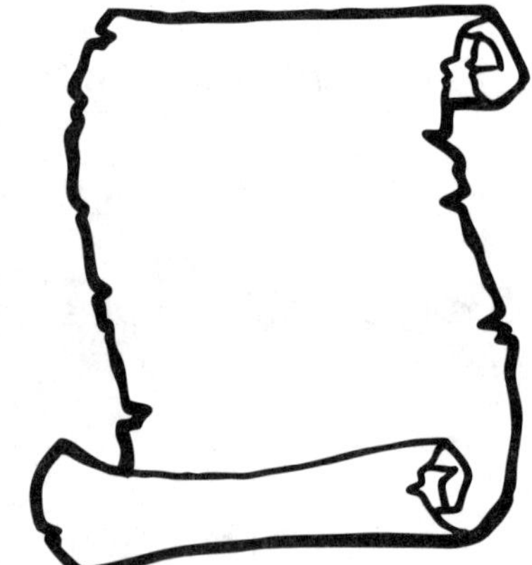

You can include any other information you would like. Be sure to give as many facts as you can.

Next, take your piece of paper and wad it up into a ball. Unfold your piece of paper, smooth it out, and then wad it up again. Do this several times until your piece of paper looks old and wrinkled. This will give your paper the appearance of paper from the past.

It is up to your teacher and the class if you decide to put these letters in a time capsule.

Fan Letters

Try your hand at writing these unique "fan" letters.

Materials:

- one piece of paper

- one paper clip

- a pencil

Directions:

1. Take a piece of paper and fold it accordion style to make a fan.

2. Think of someone famous that you admire.

3. Write the name of this person on the outside fold of your fan.

4. Then on the inside folds, write some facts about your famous person. Try to write one fact on each fold.

5. When you are finished writing, place your paper clip at the bottom of your fan to hold it together.

Feel free to add pictures or other decorations to your fan.

Once you are finished, give your fan to your teacher so she can have some "fan-tastic" decorations for the classroom!

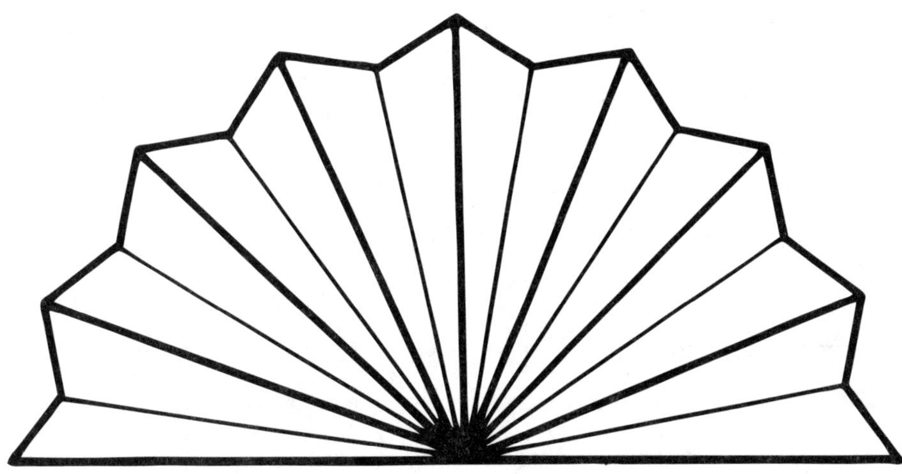

The World and Your World

The world is a very large place. Your part of the world, though not as large as the entire world, is a very important place to you.

Directions: Look at the picture below. With your teacher's help, find and color the continent on which you live. With permission from your teacher or parent, you should then use the Internet to find five facts about your continent.

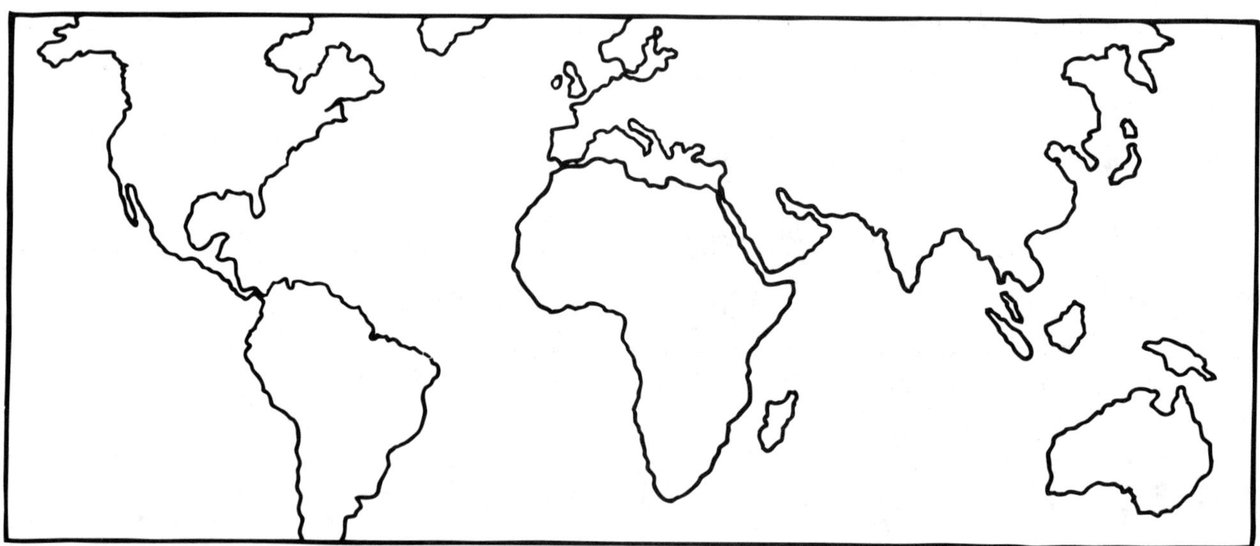

I live on the continent of ________________________________.

Here are five facts about my continent:

1. ____

2. ____

3. ____

4. ____

5. ____

Class Paper

One type of popular nonfiction writing is newspaper writing. Journalists write articles for newspapers. The articles they write are supposed to be based on facts.

Directions: Pretend you have been asked to start a class newspaper. Your first assignment is to write an article for the front page of the paper. The article must be about something that is happening at your school. Write your column in the space below.

Helpful Hint: Don't forget to give your article a title or headline. Also remember that most newspaper columns answer the five Ws: *who, what, when, where,* and *why.*

____

by _______________________________________

____

____

____

____

____

____

____

Making a Book

Nonfiction writing is some of the most enjoyable writing you will ever do. When you write nonfiction, you are learning about something. It is especially fun to write nonfiction if the topic is something you like or enjoy.

Materials:

- two pieces of construction paper
- three pieces of white paper
- pencils, crayons, markers
- stapler and staples

You will also need time on the computer or time in the library for research.

Directions: You are going to write your own nonfiction book. Your book will be five pages long (three inside pages, plus a front cover and a back cover).

Step 1

First, you will choose a topic. Choose a topic that interests you. You must choose something that is real. For example, you cannot choose unicorns as your topic.

Once you have decided on your topic, write it in the box to the right and ask your teacher if it is okay.

Step 2

Design a cover for your book. Use one piece of your construction paper and design a cover. Be sure to give your book a title. Draw and color a picture for your cover. Don't forget to include your name on the cover.

Step 3

Research your topic. With your teacher's help, look up information about your topic. Write three paragraphs about your topic. Write one paragraph on each page.

Step 4

Put your book together. Place your three pages between the cover and the second page of construction paper. Staple the book down the left edge of your paper.

Fact Collage

Materials:

- one piece of construction paper
- magazines
- glue or rubber cement
- scissors

Directions: Nonfiction writing is writing that is filled with facts. See how good you are at recognizing facts by making a fact collage.

Take a piece of construction paper and cover it with facts. Use as many magazines as you can to find your facts. Once you have found a fact in a magazine, cut it out and glue it onto your piece of construction paper. When you find another fact, add it to your piece of paper. Glue on as many facts as you can find. The facts do not have to be about the same topic.

Fact Collage

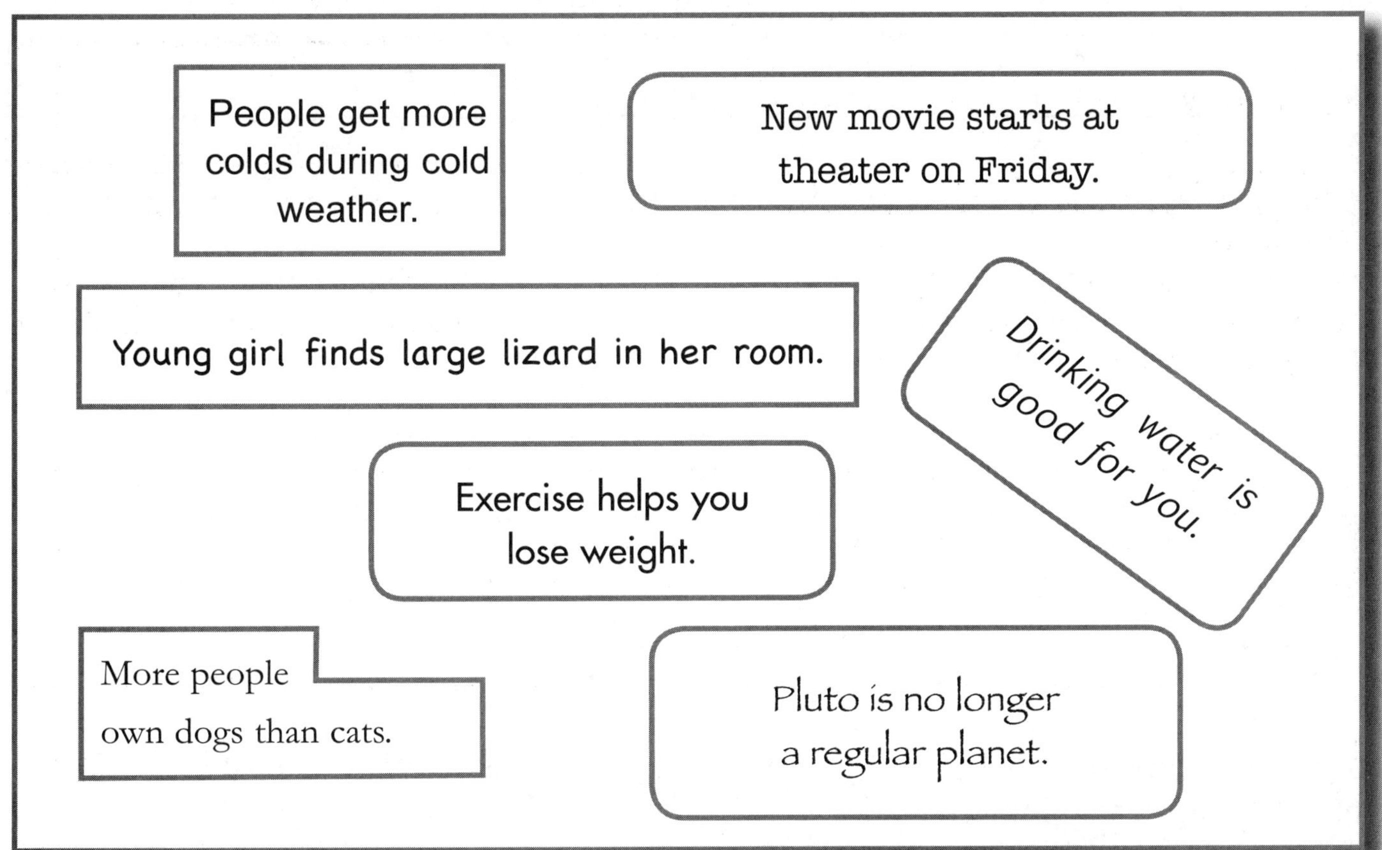

Nonfiction Poetry

Directions: Use the space below to write an acrostic poem using your name. Start by writing the letters of your name going vertically, or down the page.

Beside each letter write a word or phrase that tells something about you. The word or phrase must start with the same letter that is already written, and what you write should be true about you.

Example: Smiles at funny jokes

Always plays soccer

Makes his parents proud

Just For Fun: Since the poem is all about you, on the back of this page, draw a picture of you doing something you enjoy.

Hand Trace

Directions: Trace your hand on a piece of blank paper. Choose any animal and write the name of the animal in the palm of your hand. Research and find five facts about your animal. Write one fact on each of your fingers and thumb.

When you are finished, cut out your handprint. You can decorate your hand with rings, bracelets, etc., if you want to.

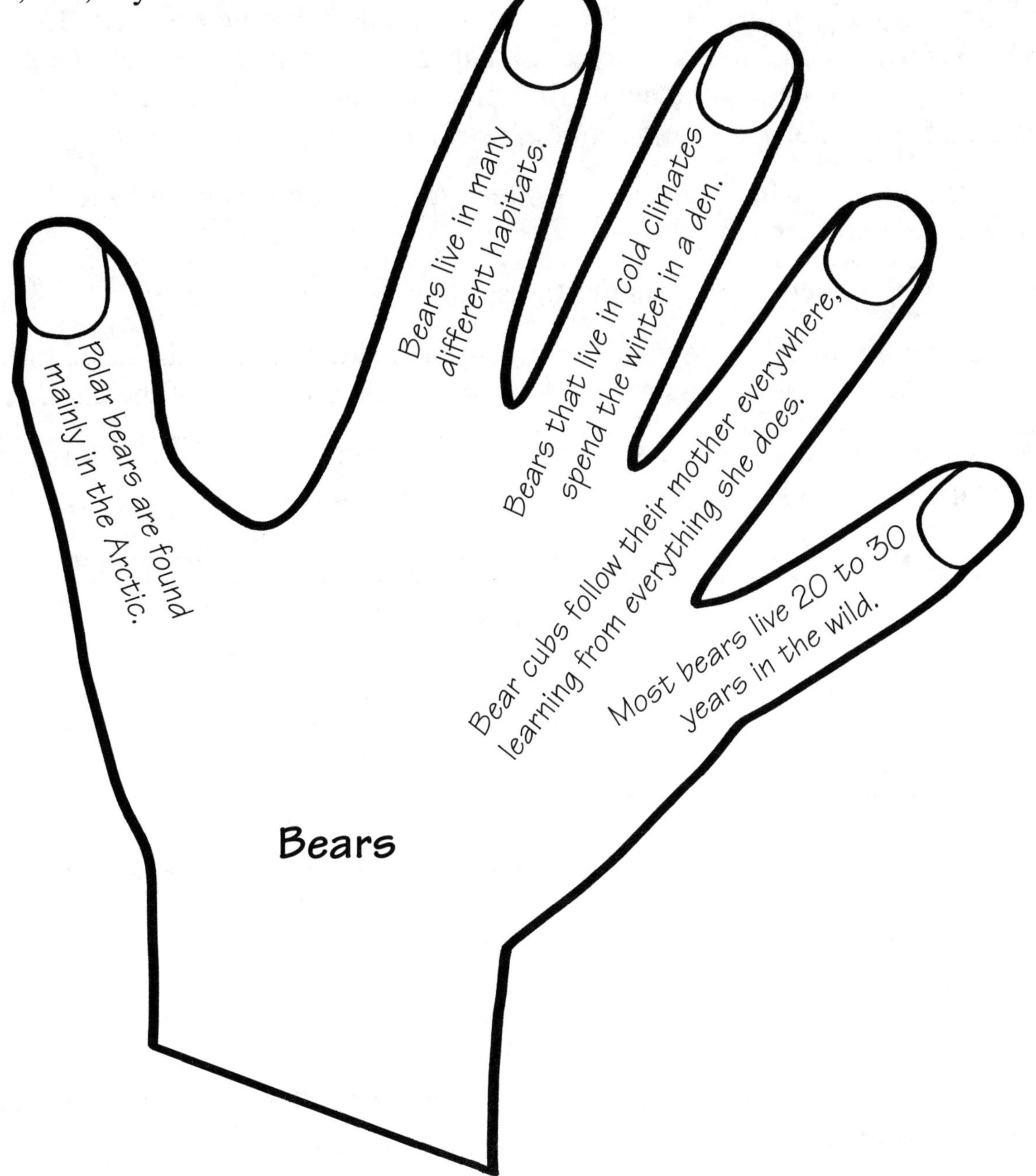

Guess Who?

Student Directions

Directions: Help your teacher make a bulletin board for the classroom.

✎ Choose someone famous from the list below or think of someone on your own. Either way, do not tell any other classmate who you choose!

✎ With the help of your teacher, research your famous someone and write five facts about this person on a piece of notebook paper. Next, take a piece of blank paper and fold it in half like a greeting card. The card should open going up. Neatly rewrite your five facts on the front of the card.

✎ Your paper needs to be folded in half like a greeting card. The card should open going up and not from the side.

✎ Write your five facts on the front of the card.

✎ Draw and color a picture of your person on the inside of the card. Write the person's name above the picture you have drawn on the inside of the card.

✎ Each student will read the facts and try to guess your person. To check the answer, he or she will open the card to find out the correct answer.

Famous People

Abraham Lincoln	Christopher Columbus
Benjamin Franklin	Pocahontas
Thomas Jefferson	Theodore Seuss Geisel (Dr. Seuss)
Martin Luther King, Jr.	Laura Ingalls Wilder
John F. Kennedy	Louis Braille
Susan B. Anthony	Sequoyah
Clara Barton	Helen Keller

Guess Who?

Sample Card

Directions: Look at the example below to see how to complete your project. Then create your own card on a piece of blank paper.

Front of the Card

1. His wife's name was Martha.

2. His home was Mount Vernon.

3. He was a general in the Revolutionary War.

4. His picture appears on the nickel and the $1 bill.

5. He was the first president of the United States.

Guess Who?

Inside of Card

George Washington!

Step by Step

Directions: Use this graph to give directions for getting ready for school each day.

First, _______________________________

____

____

Second, _______________________________

____

____

Third, _______________________________

____

____

Fourth, _______________________________

____

____

Last, _______________________________

____

____

I Do This, Then This

Directions: You have been asked to plan a birthday party for someone in your family. How will you organize it? What should be done first? What should be done after that?

Use the chart below to help you organize the party.

The Birthday Party

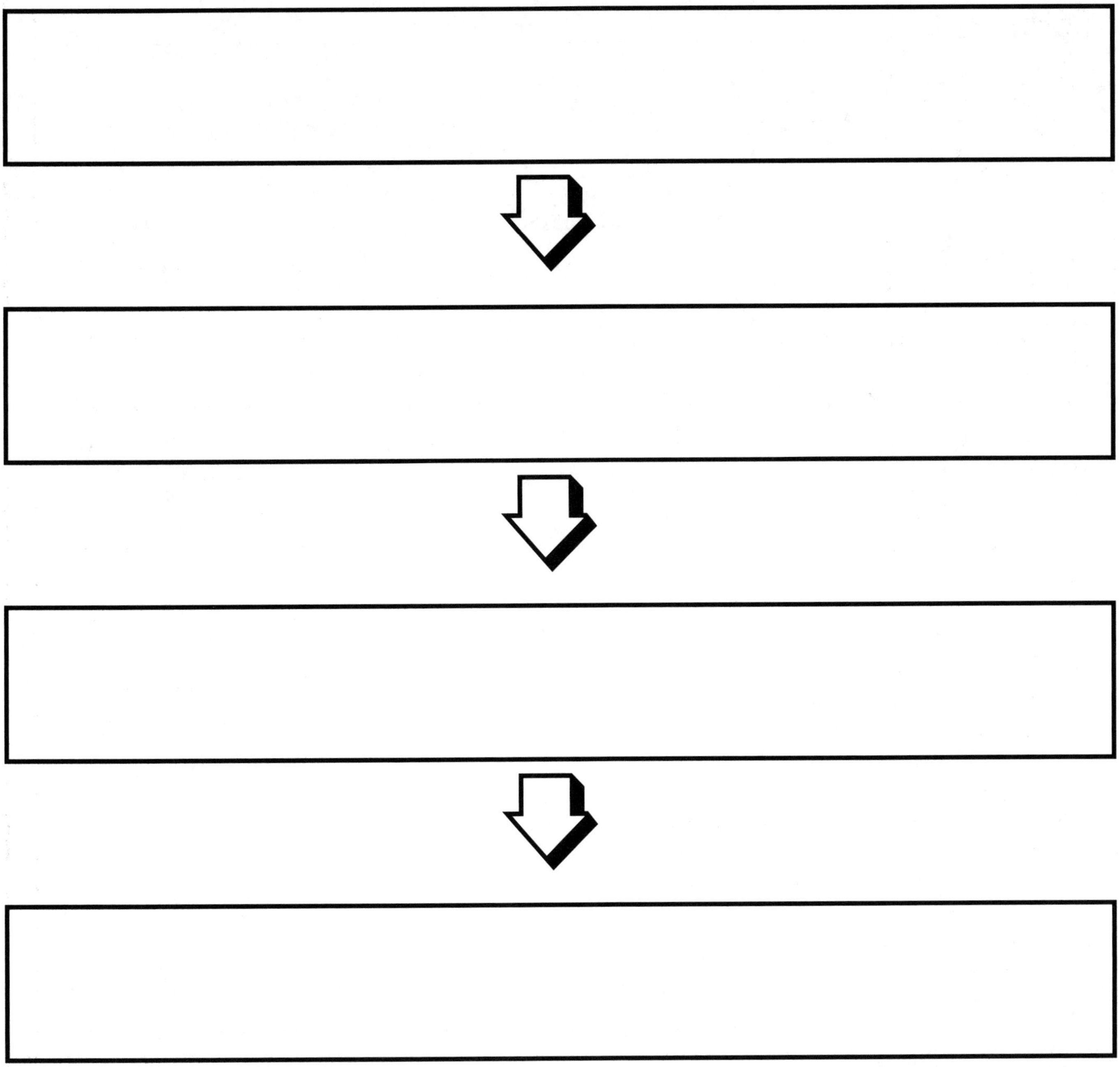

Go with the Flow

A flow chart helps keep you organized. Many big businesses use flow charts to keep workers on task and to help get the job done.

Directions: Your parents have just asked you to do the unthinkable—that's right, you have to clean your room! Use the chart below to write down the steps you need to take to get your room in beautiful shape!

Topic: ____

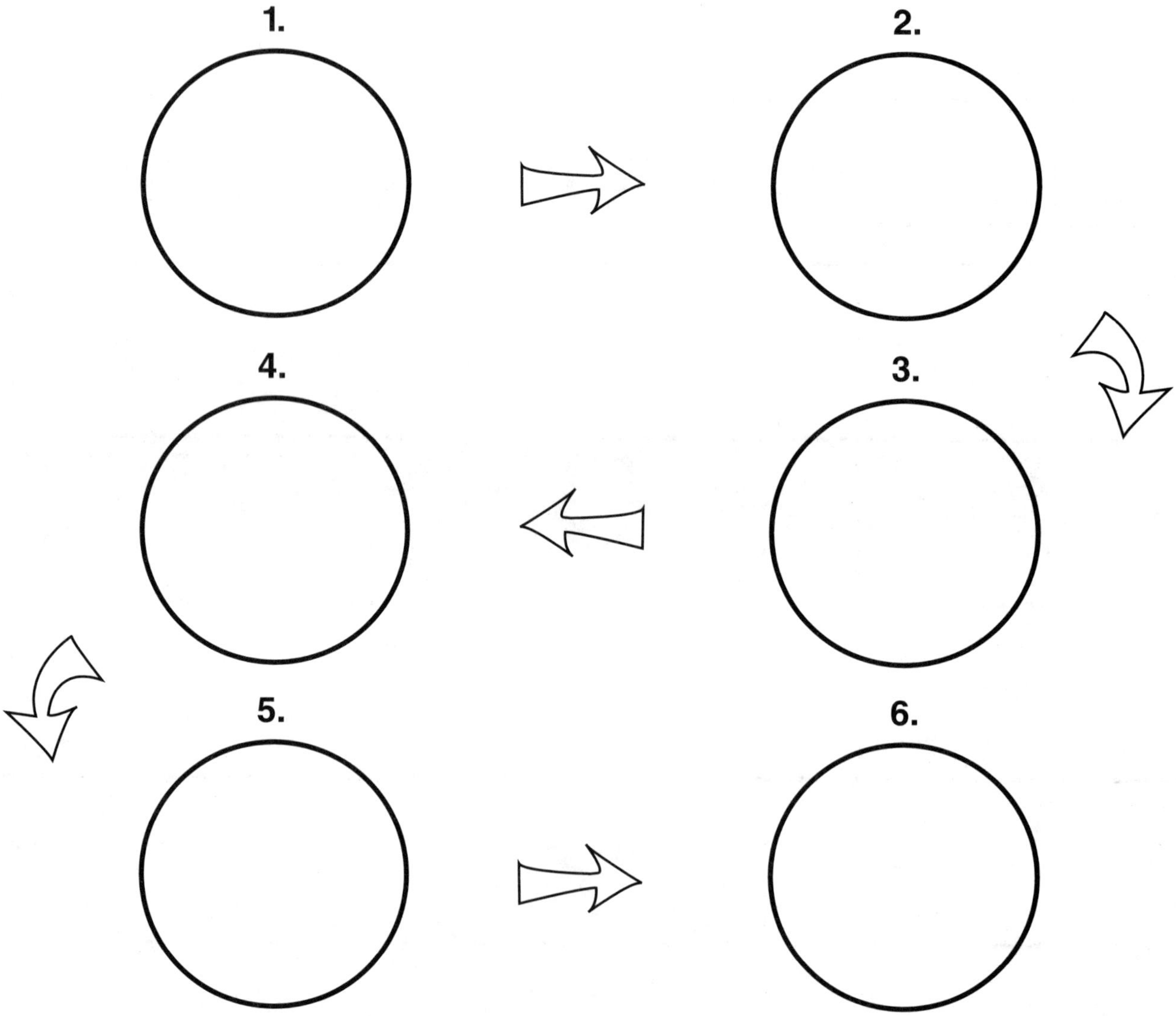

1.

2.

4.

3.

5.

6.

Just For Fun: On the back of this page, draw a picture of your room before you had to clean it!

My School Day

Most things in your life have order to them. You can practice writing about events in your life by using a sequencing chart. The word *sequence* means the order in which things occur or go.

Directions: Use the chart to write the sequence, or order, of your school day.

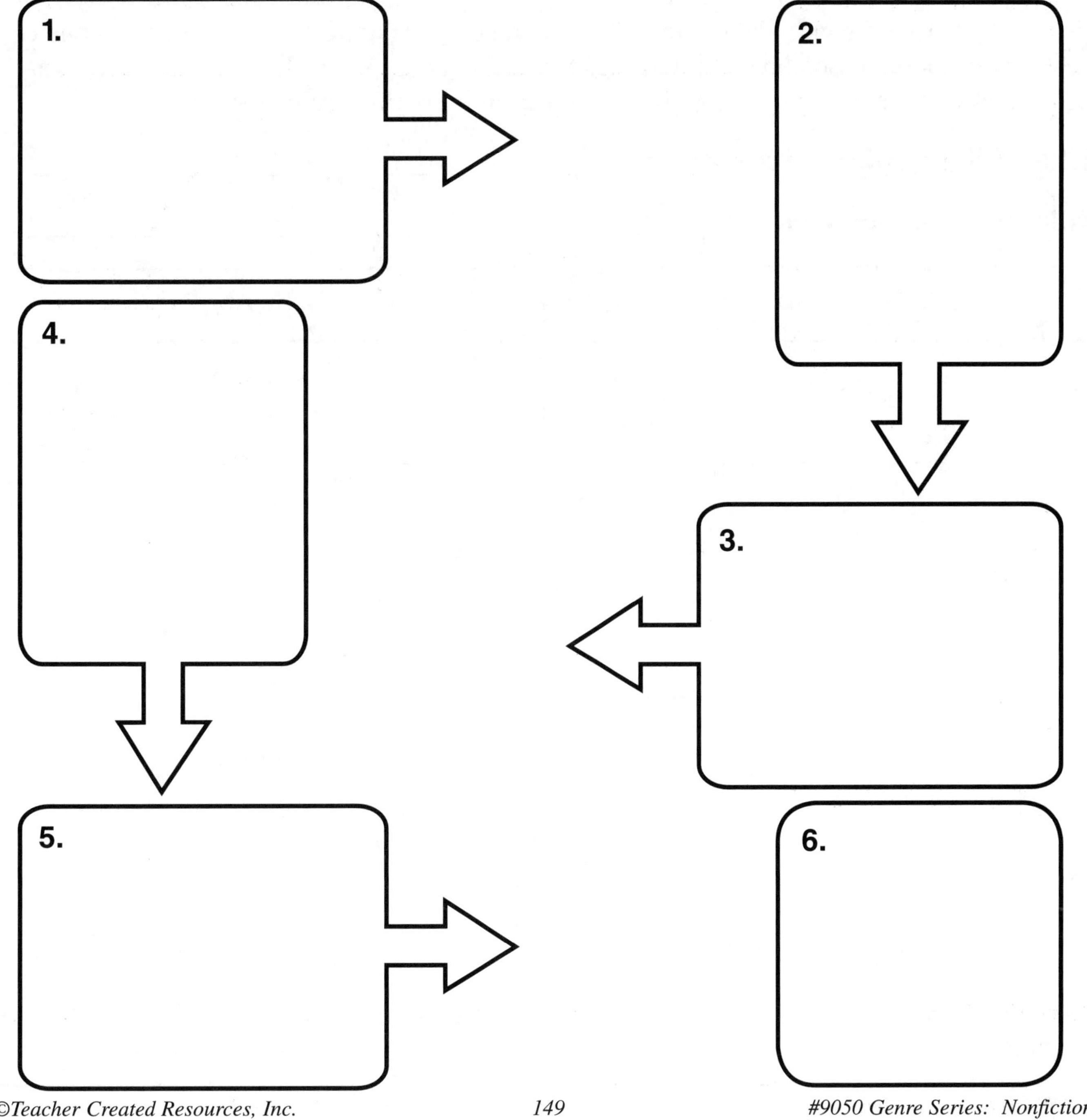

Nonfiction and Fiction

Many of your schoolbooks are nonfiction books. This means that they contain true information. Your science and social studies books are great examples of nonfiction books. However, some of your books at school contain fiction. Your reading book is a perfect example of a schoolbook that has fiction in it. Many of the stories are not based on truth (although there probably are some nonfiction stories in your reading book).

Directions: Use the chart below to compare one of your nonfiction textbooks to one of your fiction books. See how many things you can find about each book that are alike, and see how many things you can find about each book that are different.

Title of my nonfiction book: ____

Title of my fiction book: ____

Alike	**Different**

Organized Nonfiction

In nonfiction schoolbooks, the sections are organized to help readers better understand the information.

Directions: Find any section in your book. Write down the name of your book and the page number. Use the heading in that section to help you find the "main idea." Then read the section to find three details about the main idea.

My Book: ____

Page Number: _______________________________________

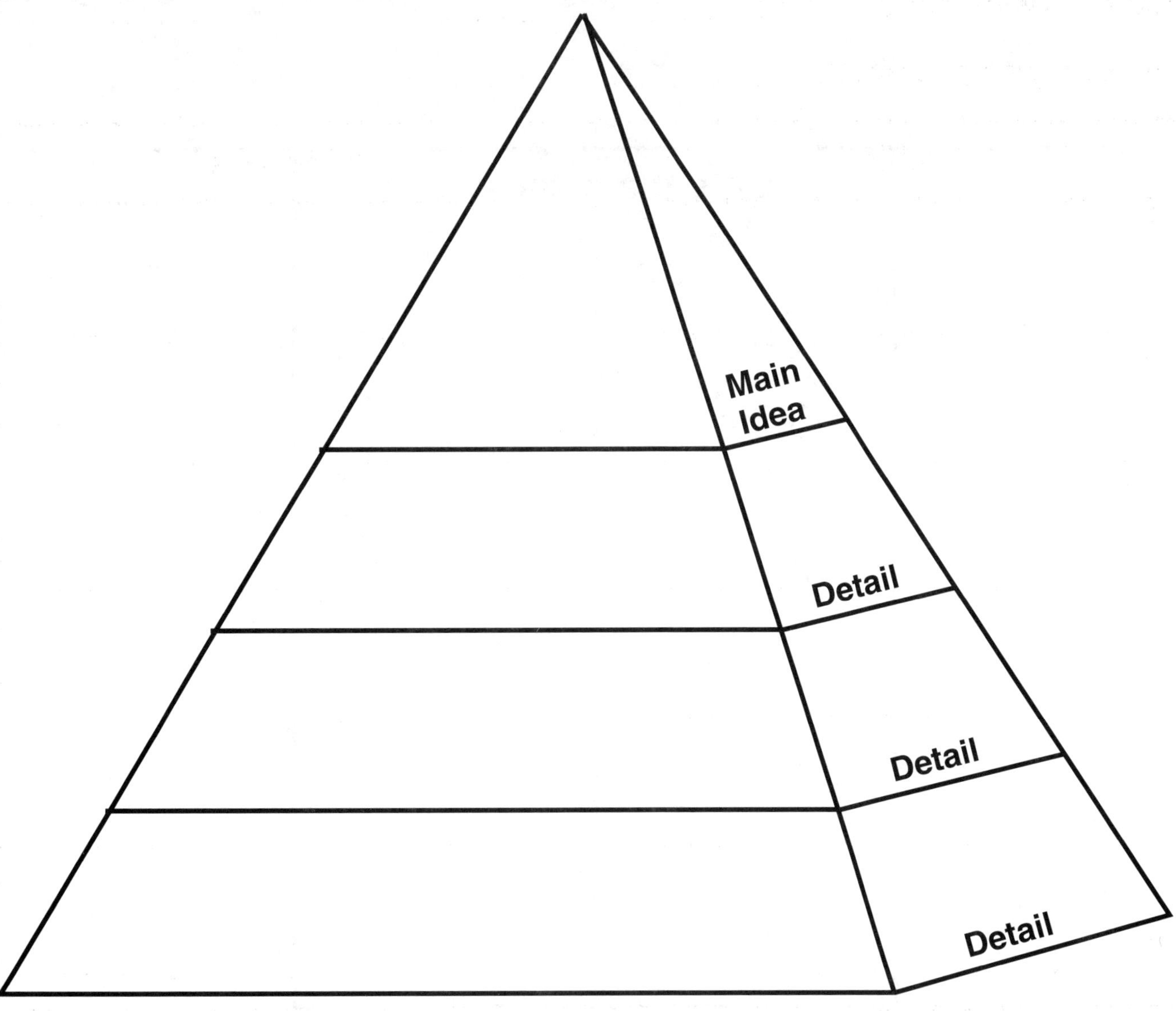

Textbook T-Bar

Directions: Use a section from your science or social studies book to complete the graph.

Helpful Hint: The main idea of a section is usually written in **bold** or **black type**. The type is also usually larger than the surrounding words.

Title of book being used: _______________________________________

Page #: ____

Main idea of section:

These are the details:

Picture Glossary

Schoolbooks often have glossaries in the back. A glossary is a dictionary of certain words that appear in that particular book.

Directions: Use a textbook from your class and look up five words in the glossary. But do not write the definition. Instead, draw a picture to represent each word!

1. _______________________________

2. _______________________________

3. _______________________________

4. _______________________________

5. _______________________________

Read It and Write

Directions: Read the following nonfiction article. Then organize what you have read on the graph below.

Neil Armstrong

Neil Armstrong was the first man to step on the moon's surface. It took Armstrong and his crew three days to reach the moon. He exited from the lunar module on July 20, 1969, and became the first man on the moon. As he stepped on the moon he said, "That's one small step for man, one giant leap for mankind." When Armstrong left the moon, more than his footsteps remained. He left a plaque that said, "Here men from the planet Earth first set foot upon the moon, July 1969 A.D. We came in peace for all mankind." An American flag was also placed on the moon that same day.

The Main Idea

Detail

Detail

Detail

Nonfiction and Fiction

Use the Venn diagram below to help compare nonfiction and fiction.

Directions: A Venn diagram is a good way to compare and contrast two things. Use the Venn diagram to compare and contrast nonfiction and fiction writing. On the sides labeled "Nonfiction" and "Fiction," only write things that can happen in those genres. Where the circles overlap, write things the two genres have in common.

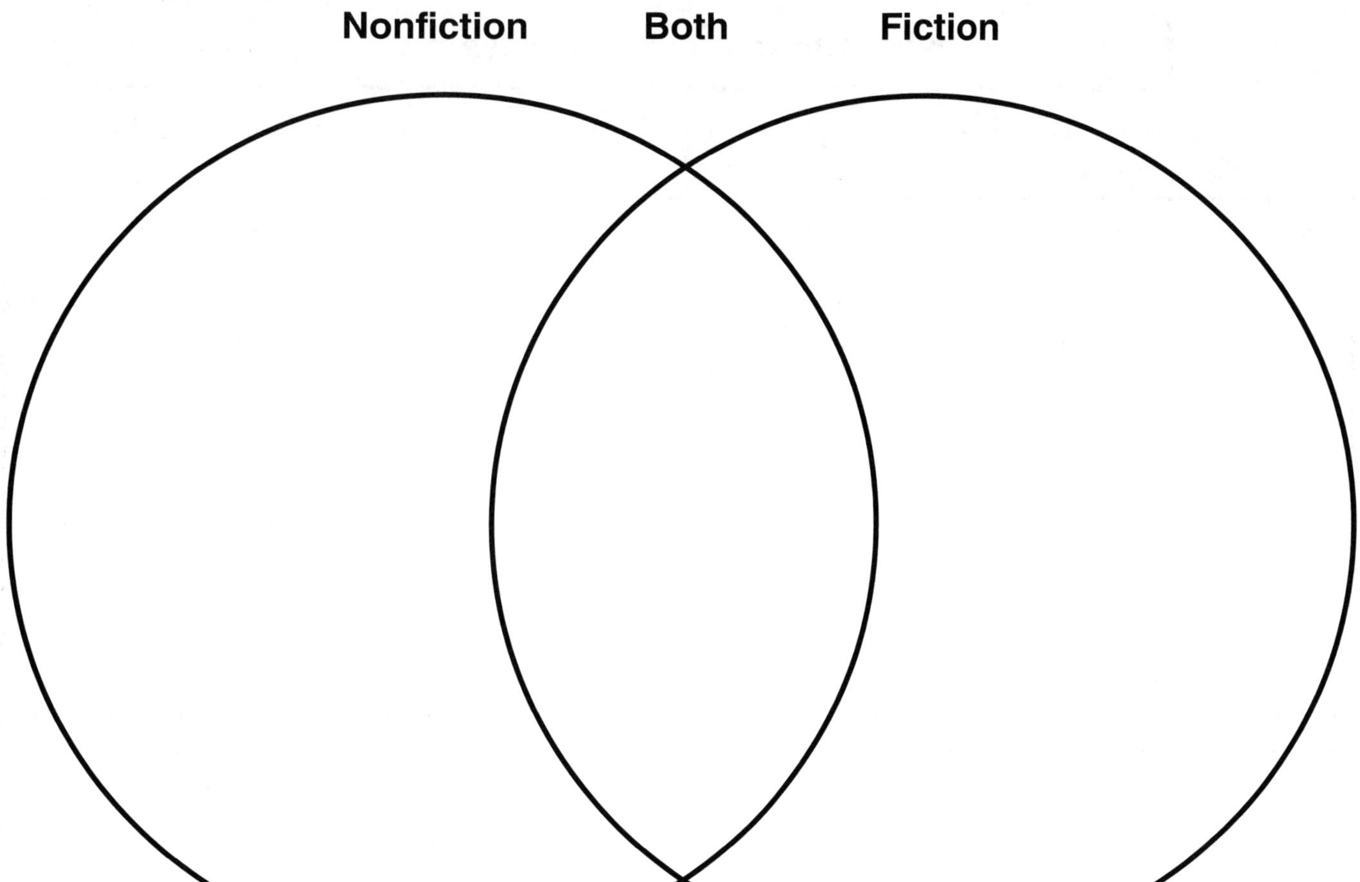

Nonfiction   **Both**   **Fiction**

Which Source?

When you want information or are doing research, one thing you have to decide is where you should go to get your information. Some people like to interview people, some people like to go to the library, others like to use the Internet.

Directions: Use the chart below to discuss the pros and cons of using the Internet for research. If something is a "pro," it is a reason *for* something. If it is a "con," it is a reason *against* something.

Example: using the library for research

      Pro: It's very quiet.   *Con:* They may not have a book you need.

Using the Internet for Research

+ PROS +	– CONS –

Organize, Then Write

Sometimes all it takes to write nonfiction is getting organized.

Directions: Look at the example to the right, and then use the blank pie graph to help you organize how you spend your day. On a separate piece of paper, write a paragraph telling how you spend your day.

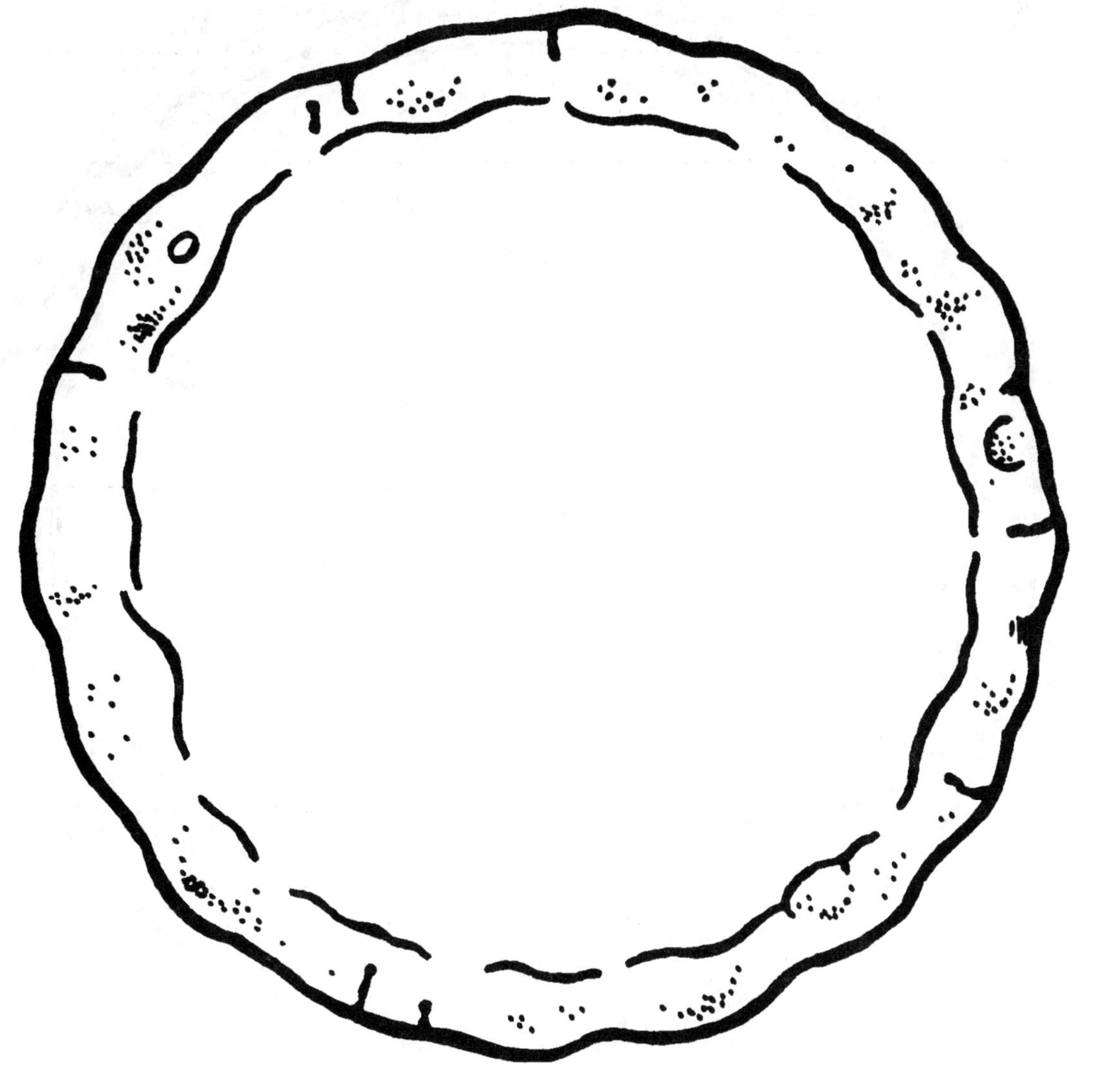

The Five Ws

Pie Graph

When you read a newspaper article it is good to look for the five Ws:

Who? • What? • When? • Where? • Why?

A good newspaper article should answer all of these questions.

Directions: Read a newspaper article. Then use the graph below to find the five Ws in your article. As you find each one, write it on the graph below.

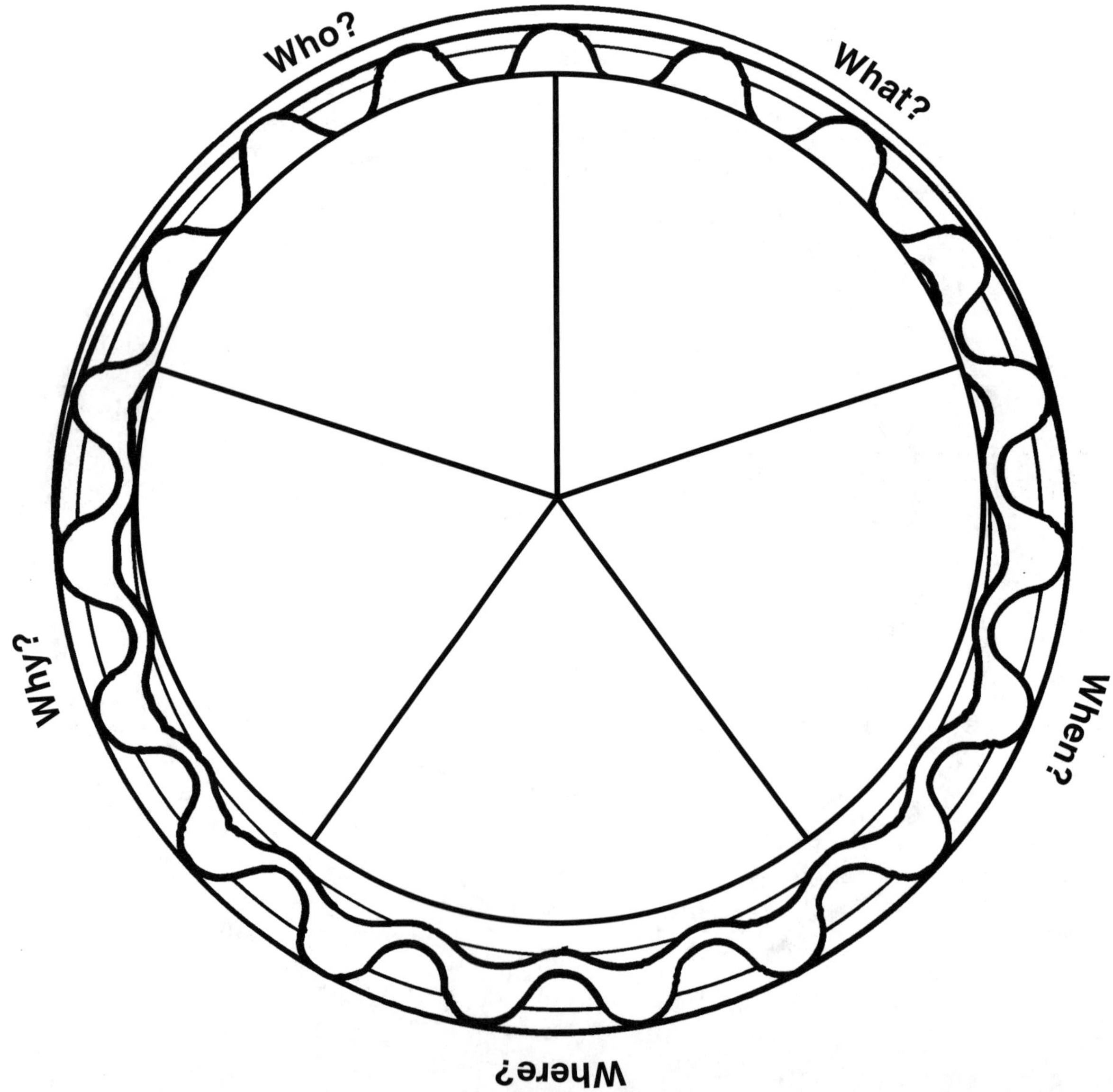

158

The Five Ws and One H

Idea Web

Directions: Use the web below to organize information from any magazine or newspaper article.

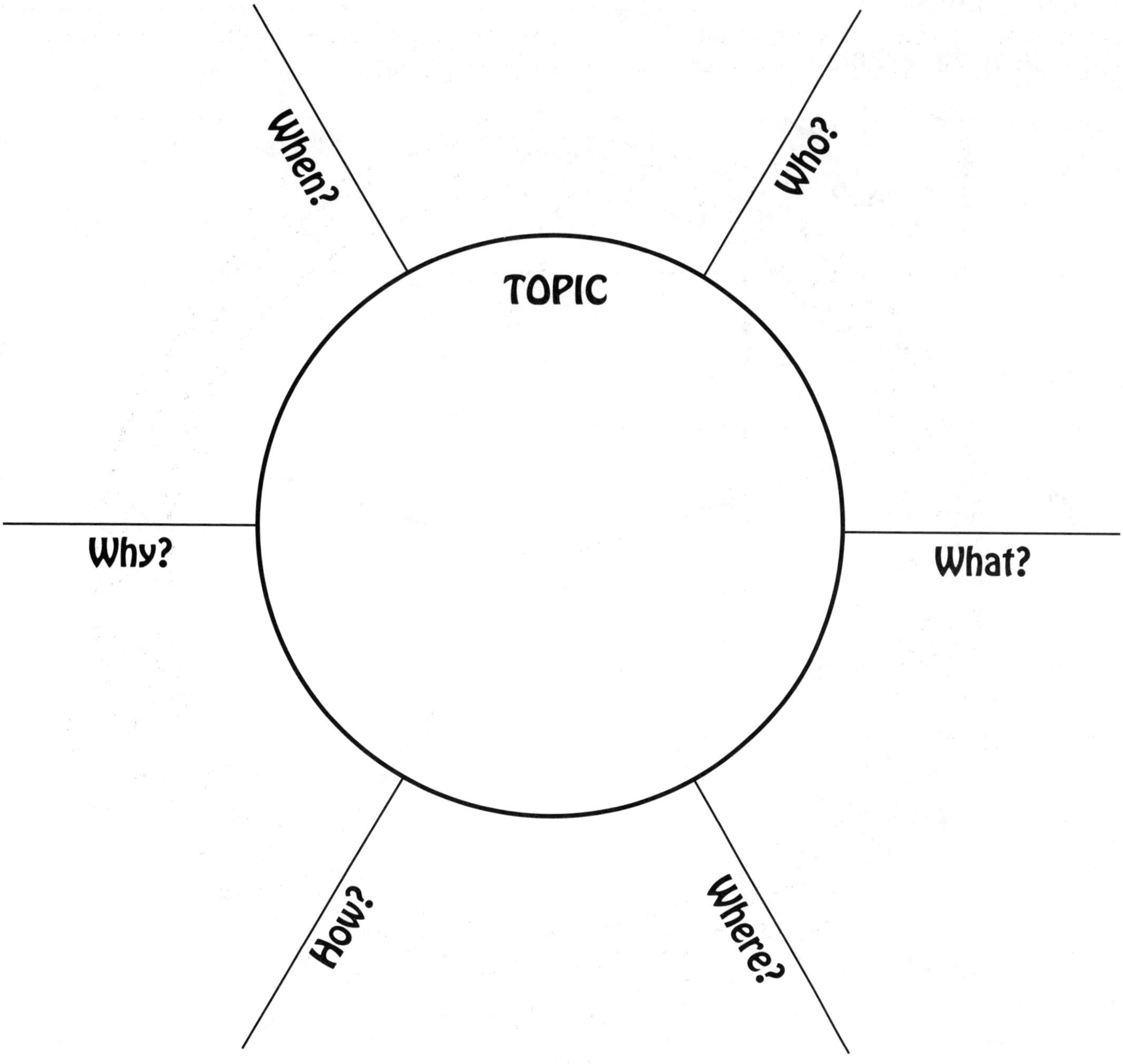

When?

Who?

TOPIC

Why?

What?

How?

Where?

Magazine Articles

Directions: Find a nonfiction article in a magazine. Read the article. Then organize the information on the graph below.

Name of the magazine: ____

Name of the article: ____

Page # of the article: ____________

What or who?	
Did what?	
When did it happen?	
Why did it happen?	
Where did it happen?	
How did it happen?	

Writing on Target

Directions: Read the nonfiction article and use the graph to help you organize the information from it. Write the article's main idea in the center of the target. Write a fact or supporting detail in each of the three rings around the center.

"I Have Not Yet Begun to Fight!"

John Paul Jones was a naval leader in the Revolutionary War. Jones was known for his attacks on British ships. Once when Jones was battling a British ship, his own ship became badly damaged. The commander on the British ship asked Jones if he would surrender. Instead of giving up, Jones answered back, "I have not yet begun to fight!" Jones and his crew ended up capturing the British ship. Instead of Jones surrendering or giving up, it was the British captain who surrendered! John Paul Jones's famous words remind people to never give up, no matter how bad something seems to be.

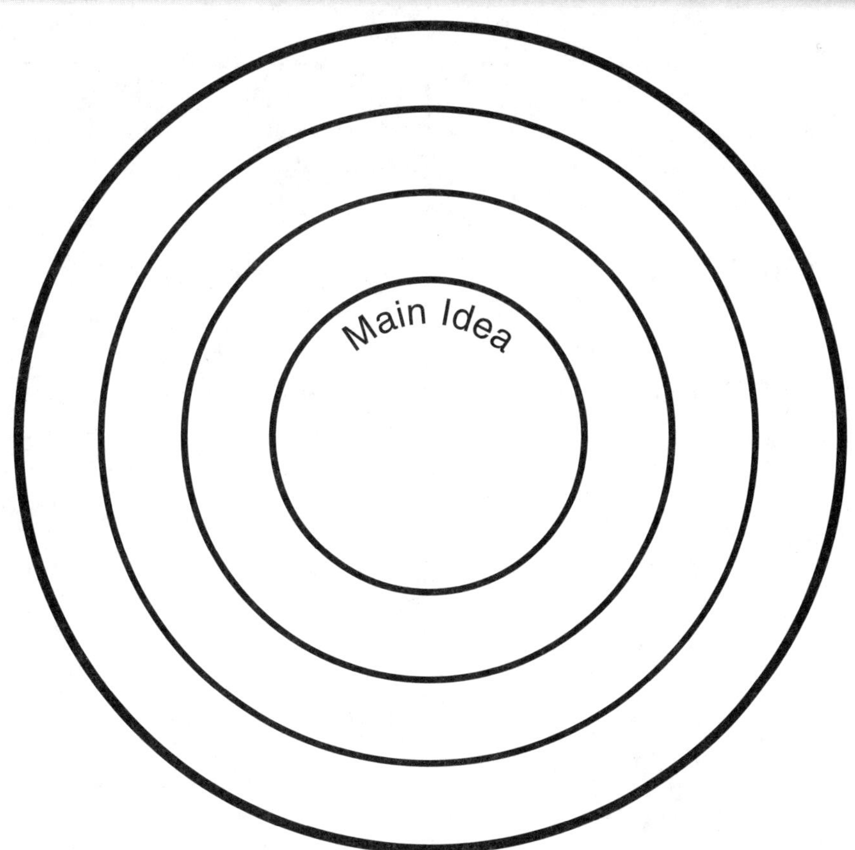

Dictionary Graph

A dictionary is an important nonfiction book. A dictionary has many parts, but one of the most important things it does is give definitions for words.

Directions: Think of two words that are new to you. Write the words on the chart below. Complete the chart and use a dictionary to check your guess.

Helpful Hint: Can't think of any "new" words? Here are some suggestions:

organism • lunar • probable • photograph • blunder • apparition

plethora • plaque • superlative • pesticide • calculator • establish

New word: _______________	**New word:** _______________
My guess: _______________	**My guess:** _______________
_______________	_______________
_______________	_______________
I guessed right! ❑	**I guessed right!** ❑
Now I know it means _______	**Now I know it means** _______
_______________	_______________
_______________	_______________

Historical Happenings

Historical nonfiction is how we learn about what has happened in the past.

Directions: Tell about a famous person or a famous event in history. How should you write it? Write about the person or the event as a comic strip! Be sure to color your pictures when you are finished.

Nonfiction Book Report

Directions: Use this page to help you organize your ideas about a book.

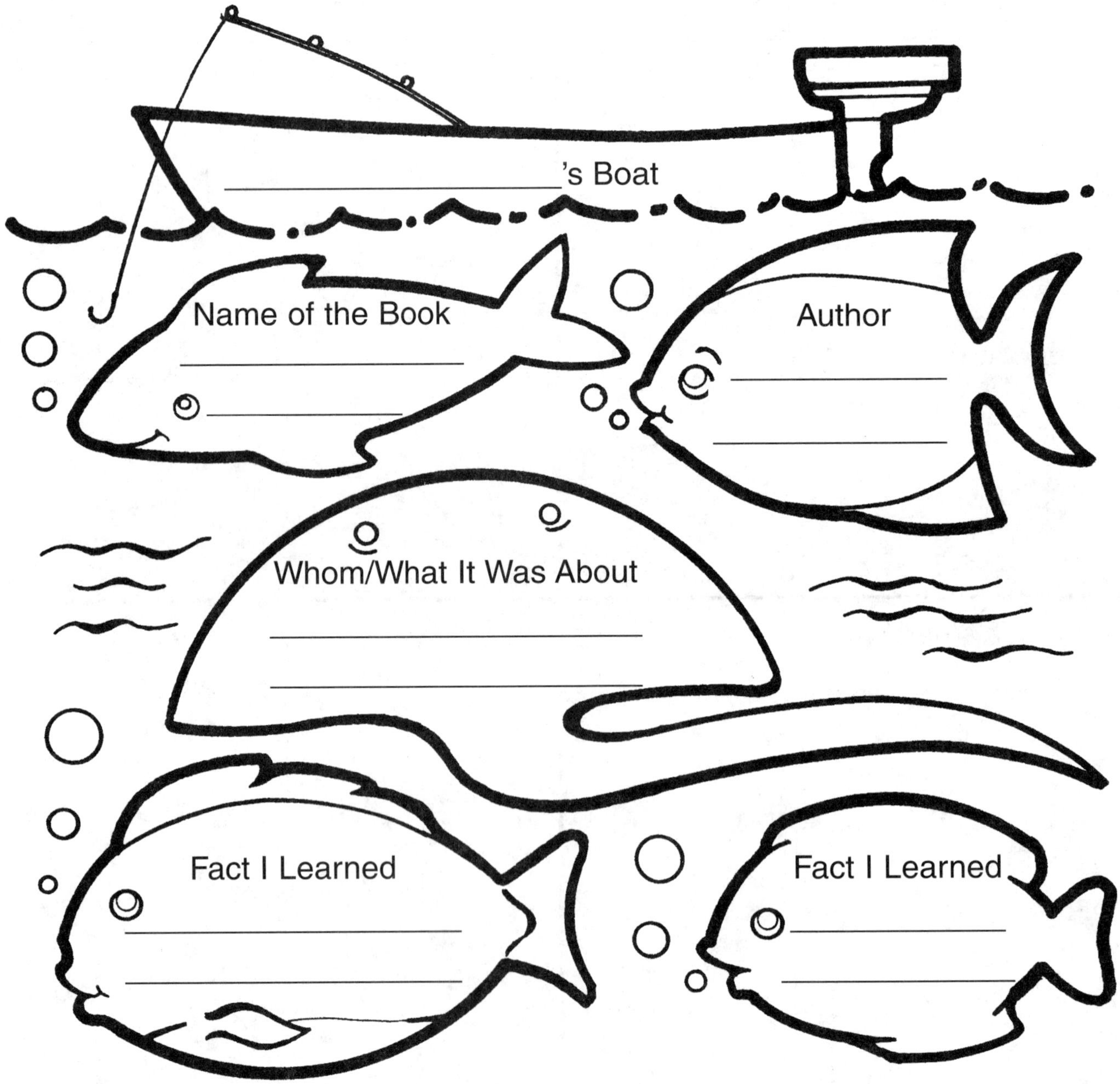

5 *Ws* and 1 *H*

Directions: Use this page to help you organize your ideas about a book or article.

Who?

What?

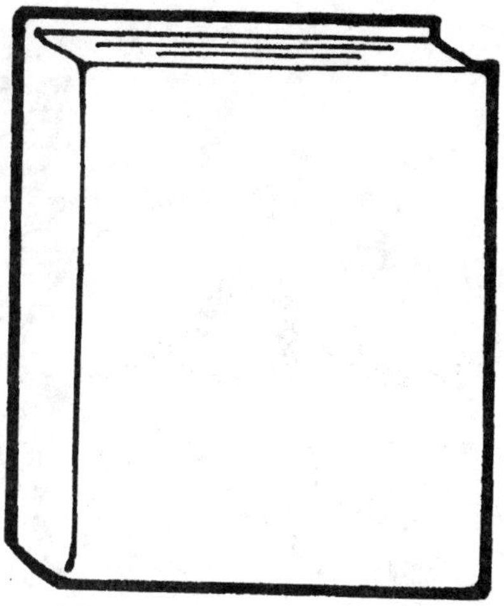

Where?

When?

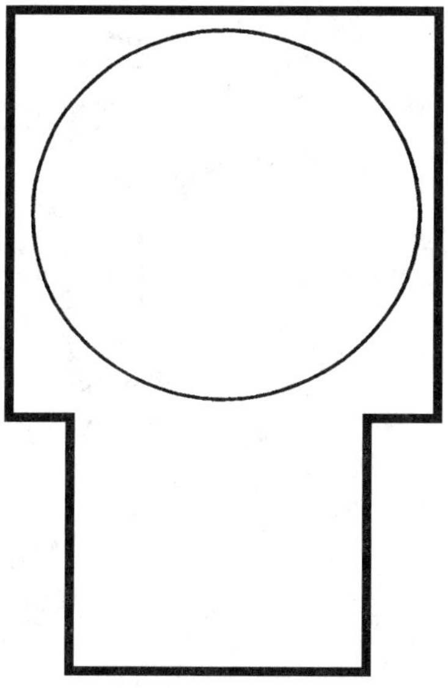

How?

Why?

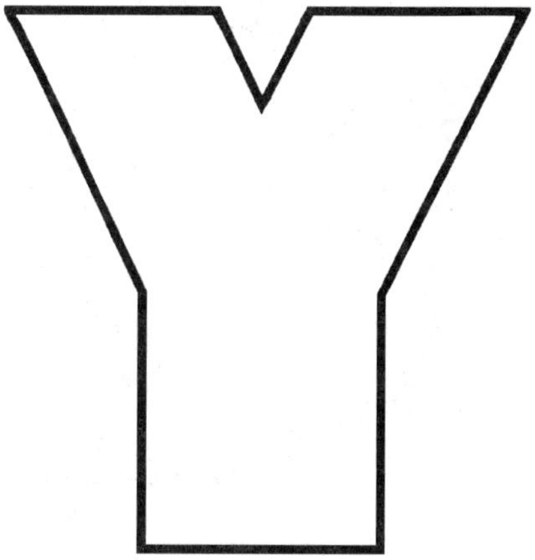

Fact Bank

Directions: Collect all the facts you can on a subject and "deposit" them in the "bank."

Topic:

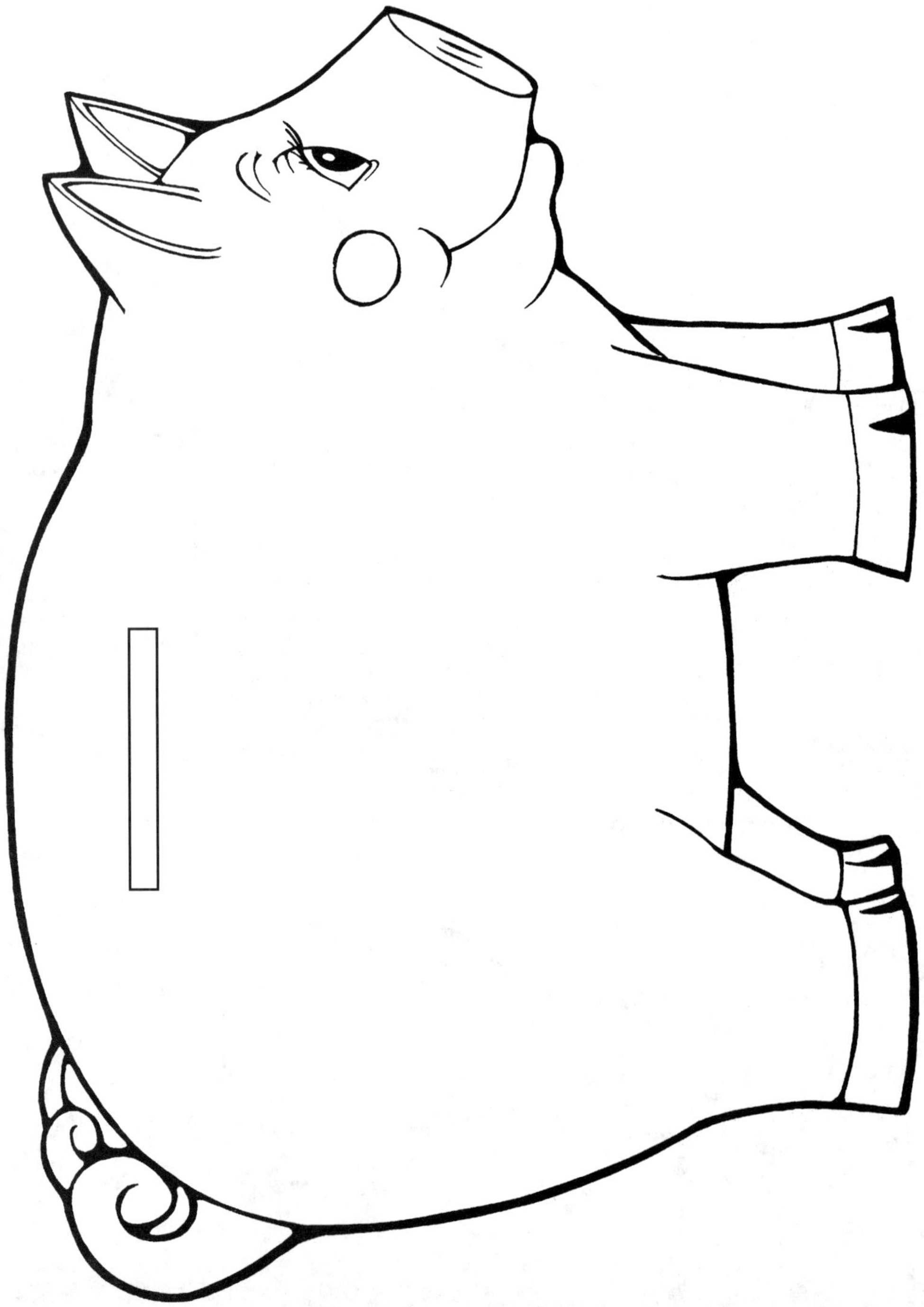

Inspector Has It!

Directions: Choose a nonfiction topic that you would like to learn more about. Some suggestions are listed below, but you can choose your own topic.

Once you have done that, write the name of the topic on the line provided.

Research your topic and write any facts you learn about your topic inside the giant magnifying glass. You can include facts that you already know.

Topic Ideas

dogs	oceans	baseball	skateboarding
seasons	school	monkeys	basketball

My topic: ____

Answer Key

Page 6

1. writing that has real people, places, and settings
2. information
3. Any of the following: textbooks, reference books, letters, diaries, and news stories.
4. Answers will vary.

Page 7

1. True
2. True
3. True
4. False
5. False
6. True
7. False
8. True

Page 9

1. Canada and Mexico
2. a passage that smoke can escape from, usually built onto a solid structure such as a house or office building
3. mainly in the Arctic
4. an eight-sided shape

Page 11

The following books could be nonfiction:

1. a book that has definitions of words
2. a book that has directions for using a computer
4. a book that gives a recipe for baking desserts
5. a book that a teacher could use in a math class
6. a book that tells about places to visit in Italy

8. a book that tells about animals that live in your part of the world

Page 13

These bears should be colored:

Bears often stand up on their back legs.

Polar bears are great swimmers.

Bears that live in cold climates spend their winters in a cave or den.

When a bear sleeps through the winter, this sleep is called hibernation.

Bears are mammals, and they have an excellent sense of smell.

Page 14

1. Yes
2. Yes
3. Yes
4. Yes
5. No
6. No
7. Yes
8. Yes

Page 15

The following books are nonfiction and should be colored:

1. *The True Story of a Pioneer*
2. *The Life of George Washington*
3. *How to Be a Great Student*
4. *Cooking for Fun*

Page 16

1. nonfiction
2. fiction
3. fiction

Answer Key *(cont.)*

Page 18

1. e	5. h
2. c	6. a
3. b	7. d
4. f	8. g

Page 20

1. nonsense
2. nonfat
3. nonstop
4. nonstick
5. nondairy

Page 21

1. fiction (red)
2. fiction (red)
3. nonfiction (yellow)
4. nonfiction (yellow)
5. fiction (yellow)
6. nonfiction (yellow)

Page 24

1. masthead
2. headline
3. caption
4. picture

Page 25

1. 1,500 miles or 2,414 km
2. because of its size
3. to protect China's border
4. Answers will vary.

Page 27

Students should only do #7. They should just write their names at the top of their papers.

Page 29

1. avenue
2. street
3. route
4. drive
5. road

Page 30

1. b, c, a
2. a, c, b
3. b, a, c
4. b, a, c

Page 31

The strips should be in this order:

1. Get your toothbrush.
2. Put toothpaste on your toothbrush.
3. Brush your teeth.
4. Just before you rinse, fill your rinsing cup with water.
5. Rinse your mouth of toothpaste.

Page 34

1. nonfiction
2. in school
3. table of contents, glossary, and index
4. the table of contents

Answer Key *(cont.)*

Page 34 *(cont.)*

5. glossary and index

6. glossary and index

7. glossary

8. Answers will vary.

Page 35

1. English

2. Parts of Speech

3. a word that takes the place of a noun

4. alphabetically

Page 36

The following books should be colored: *A to Z Guide to Cats, The Student's Almanac, Maps of Europe, The Book of Maps, The Complete Guide to Farming*

Page 37

1. Answers will vary.

2. nonfiction

3. alphabetically

4. the "L" encyclopedia

5. Answers will vary.

Page 38

1. John Adams

2. North America, South America, Asia, Africa, Antarctica, Australia, Europe

3. Atlanta

4. red, orange, yellow, green, blue, indigo, violet

5. Canada and Mexico

Page 39

1. nonfiction, because it is filled with facts

2. Answers will vary.

3. They have heavy shells covering their backs.

4. reptiles

5. more than 200 million years ago, when the dinosaurs were still alive

6. the "T" encyclopedia

Page 42

1. a type of nonfiction writing from the past

2. the Pilgrims

3. the *Mayflower*

4. a set of rules to help make the colony successful

5. Answers will vary.

6. Answers will vary.

Page 43

1. C

2. D

3. B

4. A

5. E

Page 44

1. Mr. Townes, Mr. Jones, and a dog named Scooter

2. Mr. Townes took Mr. Jones's dog.

3. Friday, August 28

Answer Key *(cont.)*

Page 44 *(cont.)*

4. in Florida and Texas

5. because the man wouldn't give the dog back to the owner

Page 45

1. Girl Saves Cat

2. Kaycee Lynn

3. It was stuck in a pond.

4. She held out a tree branch for it to use to get to safety.

5. Answers will vary.

6. Answers will vary.

Page 46

1. *The Cat's Meow*

2. people who like cats

3. people who do not like cats

4. Answers will vary.

5. Answers will vary.

Page 47

1. Poison

2. Curves, or curvy ahead

3. Stop

4. Women's (restroom)

5. Money

6. Quiet, Please!

Page 49

1. dust bunnies as pets

2. fiction

3. because it is not based on factual or real information

4. Answers will vary.

Page 50

1. d

2. c

3. b

4. a

Page 51

1. False

2. True

3. False

4. True

5. False

Page 53

1. Answers will vary.

2. Accept reasonable answers. Students might explain that these animals live so far underground that no light reaches their homes, and so the ability to see is unnecessary in their environment.

3. Students might mention the following facts: It is located in Kentucky. It is the largest cave in the world. It has 330 known passageways. It has an underground river where eyeless fish live.

Page 60

1. Science

2. Math

3. Health

4. English

5. Art

Answer Key *(cont.)*

Page 79

1. a
2. b
3. b
4. a
5. a

Page 81

1. Bears are some of the best-known animals in the world.
2. C
3. A bear's sense of smell is better than a human's.
4. Polar bears are excellent swimmers.
5. C

Page 82

1. Some people think dogs make great pets.
2. Do you have a pet dog?
3. Dogs can come in many shapes, sizes, and colors.
4. Some dogs do special jobs or services for people.
5. Many dogs shed their heavy winter coats to get ready for the warmer months.

Page 83

1. There are seven days in every week.
2. Monday starts the school week.
3. Do you think Friday is the best day of the week?

4. How wonderful it is when your birthday is on the weekend!
5. Wednesday is in the middle of the week.

Page 84

"Paul Revere's Ride" is a famous poem written by Henry Wadsworth Longfellow. (1) This poem tells the story of Paul Revere, a hero of the American Revolutionary War. (2)

Paul Revere was a silversmith who, on the night before the Battle of Lexington and Concord, rode across the Massachusetts countryside warning that the British troops were moving toward them. (3)

"One if by land, and two if by sea" are the words Longfellow used to describe the signal Paul Revere would use. (4) Revere watched a church tower to find the signal. (5) One light in the church tower meant the troops were coming by land. (6) What do you think two lights meant? (7)

Because Revere made his famous ride, everyone was warned that night. (8)

The next day, they were ready to fight the British. (9) How brave Paul Revere must have been to make his famous ride! (10)

Page 85

1. Being a good runner takes lots of practice.○
2. Ⓐmarathon is a long race in which many people run at the same time.

Answer Key *(cont.)*

Page 85 *(cont.)*

3. The (B)oston Marathon is a well-known race.

4. (R)unners must drink lots of water.

5. Running is a good type of exercise.

6. A runner must wear a good pair of running shoes(.)

7. (I)f you plan to run in a marathon, you must train for the event.

8. How wonderful it would be to win a marathon(!)

Page 86

Can you guess what happened to me while I was babysitting? I <u>was</u> watching this cute little girl named Kara. She wanted to play a <u>game</u>. While <u>I</u> was in the living room setting up a game for us to play, Kara snuck into the kitchen. <u>She</u> opened a bottle of syrup and poured it all over the entire kitchen!

It took me three hours to get the icky mess off of everything<u>.</u> Luckily, by the time Kara's mom came home, everything was clean, but things did still smell a little <u>sweet</u>.

Kara's mom paid me my money, but it was the hardest <u>money</u> I ever earned.

Page 87

1. Basketball
2. Butterflies
3. Cats

4. Congress
5. Insects
6. Movies
7. Pilgrims
8. Space
9. Sports
10. Tenne*ssee

Page 91

The following words should be circled:

1. Chloe
2. Kayla Beth
3. Gage
4. Brett
5. Sandra
6. Kaycee
7. Emilee
8. Daniel

Page 93

1. Dolphins	4. is
2. have	5. Catfish
3. Worms	6. are

Page 94

1. animals	5. little
2. first	6. easy
3. were	7. because
4. has	8. back

Answer Key *(cont.)*

Page 95

1. Our friends are very nice.

2. Their friends are nice, too.

3. There was a sale on juice at the grocery store.

4. Do you want to go, or do you want to stay?

5. For her birthday she got two puppies.

Page 97

1. American black bears can actually be black, brown, or white!

2. There are many types of bears, including polar bears, panda bears, and black bears.

3. Bears' strong teeth can grab, crush, and chew their food.

4. Polar bears can be found in Alaska, Canada, Russia, Denmark, and Norway.

5. Many bears can climb, run, and swim.

6. Bears will protect their cubs from wolves, mountain lions, and humans.

7. A female bear can have one, two, or three cubs at a time.

8. Polar bears like ice, snow, and cold weather.

Page 100

1. The jungle can be a scary place.

2. It often rains a lot in the jungle.

3. Would you like to go and visit the jungle?

4. I bet you would see snakes, monkeys, and lizards in the jungle.

5. One famous, funny, and fantastic book about jungle life is called *The Jungle Book.*

6. It is possible to survive being lost in the jungle.

7. In the jungle, monkeys swing from vine to vine.

8. I wish I could swing from a vine like a monkey.

Page 104

The balloons next to these statements should be colored:

1. Encyclopedias are a type of nonfiction.

2. Nonfiction can be described as writing that is true or not make-believe.

3. The opposite of nonfiction is fiction.

4. A nonfiction writer gives information to the reader.

5. Historical documents are an example of nonfiction.

6. A letter written by the Wicked Witch of the East would not be an example of nonfiction writing.

Page 105

1. a   5. b

2. a   6. b

3. a   7. b

4. b   8. b

Answer Key *(cont.)*

Page 108

1. Fact
2. Fact
3. Not a Fact
4. Not a Fact
5. Not a Fact
6. Fact
7. Fact
8. Not a Fact
9. Not a Fact
10. Not a Fact

Page 109

1. b
2. a
3. a
4. a
5. a
6. a
7. b
8. b

Page 110

Real Event/Nonfiction:

It will rain this year

A teacher will teach your class.

The sun will shine this year.

You will have a birthday this year.

You will eat a meal this week.

Not a Real Event/Fiction:

An alien will come today and take you back to his planet.

A talking dog will teach your class.

The moon will decide to take a vacation at the beach.

Goldilocks and the three bears will invite you over for some porridge.

A fairy godmother will come and offer you three wishes.

Page 112

Color the following:

1. Reference books are a form of nonfiction.
3. Directions that tell you how to bake a pie are nonfiction.
4. Encyclopedias are nonfiction and are organized alphabetically.
5. A true story about a bear in the wilderness would be nonfiction.

Page 113

1. 29,028 feet (8,848 m)
2. There is not enough oxygen up that high; the air is very thin.
3. Edmund Hillary and Tenzing Norgay
4. 1975
5. Answers will vary.
6. Answers will vary.

Page 115

1. e
2. d
3. b
4. a
5. d

Answer Key *(cont.)*

Page 116

1. a Cherokee Native American who created a written alphabet
2. Tennessee
3. The Cherokee people needed a written alphabet.
4. 85
5. Answers will vary.

Page 117

Cookies that should be colored:

1. Over 7 billion chocolate chip cookies are eaten each year.
3. Ruth Wakefield invented the chocolate chip cookie.
5. Chocolate chip cookies were created in 1930.
8. Ruth Wakefield ran the Toll House Inn.

Page 119

1. true
2. Fiction
3. directions
4. newspaper
5. Nonfiction
6. diary
7. Encyclopedias
8. alphabetically

Page 122

The following cats should be colored:

1. Nonfiction writing is filled with facts.
3. An encyclopedia is a type of nonfiction writing.
4. Encyclopedias are organized alphabetically.
5. Dictionaries are a type of nonfiction writing.
7. The opposite of nonfiction is fiction.

Bibliography

Foster, Ruth. *Take Five Minutes: Fascinating Facts and Stories for Reading and Critical Thinking.* Teacher Created Resources, 2001.

Morgan, Sally. *Animal Lives: Bears.* Teacher Created Resources, 2004.

Morgan, Sally. *Animal Lives: Tortoises and Turtles.* Teacher Created Resources, 2004.

Petersen, Casey Null. *Graphic Organizers, GradesÅ K–3.* Teacher Created Resources, 2004.